INDIGENOUS LIFE AFTER THE CONQUEST

memoria n̄ tlahcoya tlacala
suli yq̄ na inicihuits deis 5 ḡa̅s
q̄ na moxadco tan pable ———

⊕ ⊕ ✚ ⊕ ✚ ⊕ ✚ ⊕ ✚ ✚ | ⊕
⊕ ⊕ ⊙

axcal ne sy aiq̄ De sf̄ulioegui
ce fuecon tlacdlaquili nakacli
peso huer no ne peso r̄ e fuecyei
te ni glaciq̄ q̄ ta viar ——— 12 p̄
                              3 tp̄

⊕ ⊕ ⊕ ⊕ ⊕ ⊕ ⊕ ⊕ ⊕ ⊕ ⊕ ⊕

rixi.iixt 1658 a
⊕ ✚ ✚ ✚ ✚ ✚ ⊕
⊕ ⊕ ✚ ✚ ✚ ⊕ ⊕

axcal fuebes a
ponua con tla
Te So uen cax
no tepeso r̄

teston
⊕ ⊕ ⊕ ⊕ ✚ ⊕
⊕ ⊕ ⊙ ⊙ ⊙

INDIGENOUS LIFE AFTER THE CONQUEST

The De la Cruz Family Papers of Colonial Mexico

Caterina Pizzigoni and Camilla Townsend

The Pennsylvania State University Press
University Park, Pennsylvania

Library of Congress Cataloging-in-Publication Data

Names: Pizzigoni, Caterina, compiler. | Townsend, Camilla, 1965– compiler. |
    Cruz (Family : approximately 1620– Cruz, Pedro de la, approximately
    1620–1675), creator. | Cruz, Pedro de la, approximately 1620–1675,
    author. | Cruz, Juan de la, approximately 1640–1691, author.
Title: Indigenous life after the conquest : the De la Cruz family papers of
    colonial Mexico / Caterina Pizzigoni and Camilla Townsend [compilers].
Other titles: Latin American originals ; 16.
Description: University Park, Pennsylvania : The Pennsylvania State
    University Press, [2021] | Series: Latin american originals ; 16 | Includes
    bibliographical references and index. | English translations of originals
    in Nahuatl and Spanish; one document includes the original Nahuatl.
Summary: "Examines a rare set of family documents from central Mexico,
    originally written in Nahuatl, from the seventeenth to the early
    nineteenth century. Illustrates a complex indigenous world, with
    the challenges and opportunities of life within the Spanish colonial
    system"—Provided by publisher.
Identifiers: LCCN 2021000212 | ISBN 9780271088136 (paperback)
Subjects: LCSH: Cruz family—Archives. | Cruz, Pedro de la, approximately
    1620–1675—Archives. | Cruz, Juan de la, approximately 1640–1691—
    Archives. | Nahuas—Mexico—Tepemaxalco—History—17th century—
    Sources. | Nahuas—Mexico—Tepemaxalco—Social life and customs—
    17th century—Sources. | Tepemaxalco (Mexico)—History—17th
    century—Sources. | Tepemaxalco (Mexico)—Social life and customs—
    17th century—Sources. | Tepemaxalco (Mexico)—Church history—17th
    century—Sources.
Classification: LCC F1221.N3 P59 2021 | DDC 972/.4802—dc23
LC record available at https://lccn.loc.gov/2021000212

Published by The Pennsylvania State University Press,
University Park, PA 16802-1003

The Pennsylvania State University Press is a member of the Association of
University Presses.

It is the policy of The Pennsylvania State University Press to use acid-free
paper. Publications on uncoated stock satisfy the minimum requirements
of American National Standard for Information Sciences—Permanence of
Paper for Printed Library Material, ANSI Z39.48-1992.

This book is dedicated to the memory of Jim Lockhart, without whom it would never have been written.

CONTENTS

Latin American Originals (LAO) is a series of primary-source texts on colonial Latin America. LAO volumes are accessible editions of texts translated into English—most of them for the very first time. Of the sixteen volumes now in print, nine illuminate aspects of the Spanish invasions in the Americas during the long century of 1494–1614. The other seven take the series in varied and exciting directions, from the spiritual conquest to medical science; the present volume acts as a bridge between the invasion-era volumes and those exploring the mid- and late colonial periods.

Taken in the chronological order of their primary texts, *Of Cannibals and Kings* (LAO 7) comes first. It presents the earliest written attempts to describe Native American cultures, offering striking insight into how the first Europeans in the Americas struggled from the very start to conceive a "New World." *The Native Conquistador* (LAO 10) tells the story of the (in)famous Spanish Conquest expeditions into Mexico and Central America from 1519 to 1524—but from the startlingly different perspective of an indigenous dynasty, with Ixtlilxochitl, ruler of Tetzcoco, the alternative leading protagonist, as recounted by his great-great-grandson.

Next, chronologically, are LAOs 2, 1, and 9. *Invading Guatemala* shows how reading multiple accounts of conquest wars (in this case, Spanish, Nahua, and Maya versions of the Guatemalan conflict of the 1520s) can explode established narratives and suggest a more complex and revealing conquest story. *Invading Colombia* challenges us to view the difficult Spanish invasion of Colombia in the 1530s as more representative of conquest campaigns than the better-known assaults on the Aztec and Inca Empires. It complements *The Improbable Conquest*, which presents letters written between 1537 and 1556 by Spaniards struggling—with a persistence that is improbable indeed—to found a colony along the hopefully named Río de la Plata.

Contesting Conquest (LAO 12) adds intriguingly to that trio, offering new perspectives on Nueva Galicia's understudied early history. Indigenous witnesses and informants, their voices deftly identified, selected, and presented, guide us through the grim, messy tale of repeated efforts at conquest and colonization from the late 1520s through 1545.

LAOs 11, 3, 4, and 16 (this volume) all explore aspects of the aftermath and legacy of the invasion era. *The History of the New World* offers the first English translation since 1847 of part of a 1565 Italian book that, in its day, was a best seller in five languages. The merchant-adventurer Girolamo Benzoni mixes sharp observations and sympathy for indigenous peoples with imaginary tales and wild history, influencing generations of early modern readers and challenging modern readers to sort out fact from fable. *The Conquest on Trial* features a fictional indigenous embassy filing a complaint in a court in Spain—the Court of Death. The first theatrical examination of the conquest published in Spain, it effectively condenses contemporary debates on colonization into one dramatic package. It contrasts well with *Defending the Conquest*, which presents a spirited, ill-humored, and polemic apologia for the Spanish Conquest, written in 1613 by a veteran conquistador.

The present volume chronologically follows those three. In *Indigenous Life After the Conquest*, Caterina Pizzigoni and Camilla Townsend, two master scholars of Nahua history and culture, present the papers of a Nahua family, showing how family members navigated the gradual changes and challenges that swept central Mexico in the century after the dramatic upheaval of invasion and conquest. Through indigenous eyes we see how a new order was built, contested, shaped, and reconfigured by Nahuas themselves.

LAO 16 dovetails in many ways with volumes 13, 6, 5, and 8—which explore aspects of Spanish efforts to implant Christianity in the Americas. Chronologically, *To Heaven or to Hell* leads the pack, presenting the first complete English translation of a book by Bartolomé de Las Casas. Originally published in 1552, his *Confessionary for Confessors*—soon overshadowed by his famous *Very Brief Account of the Destruction of the Indies*—was initially just as controversial; conquistadors and other Spaniards were outraged by its demand that they themselves be effectively made subject to the spiritual conquest in the Americas.

Gods of the Andes presents the first English edition of a 1594 manuscript describing Inca religion and the campaign to convert native Andeans. Its Jesuit author is surprisingly sympathetic to preconquest beliefs and practices, viewing them as preparing Andeans for the arrival of the new faith. *Forgotten Franciscans* casts new light on the spiritual conquest and the conflictive cultural world of the Inquisition in sixteenth-century Mexico. Both LAO 6 and 5 expose wildly divergent views within the Spanish American church on native religions and how to replace them with Christianity. Complementing those two volumes by revealing the indigenous side to the same process, *Translated Christianities* presents religious texts translated from Nahuatl and Yucatec Maya. Designed to proselytize and ensure the piety of indigenous parishioners, these texts show how such efforts actually contributed to the development of local Christianities.

LAOs 14 and 15 take the series in bold new directions. *To the Shores of Chile* presents the "Journal and History" of a Dutch expedition to Chile, bringing to seven the number of languages from which LAO sources have been translated. Extending the series into a new region of the Americas, it opens up a new perspective on European-indigenous interaction, colonization, and global competition in the age of empire. *Baptism Through Incision* takes the LAO series later in time and into medical history, using an eighteenth-century Guatemalan case study to explore the fascinating intersections between faith and science in the early modern world. This first English publication and presentation of an eye-opening 1786 treatise on performing cesareans on pregnant women at the moment of their death explores anew many of the themes threaded through previous series volumes—empire, salvation, the female body, and knowledge as an American battleground.

The source texts in LAO volumes are colonial-era rare books or archival documents, written in European or Mesoamerican languages. LAO authors are historians, anthropologists, and scholars of literature who have developed a specialized knowledge that allows them to locate, translate, and present these texts in a way that contributes to scholars' understanding of the period, while also making them readable for students and nonspecialists. There has never before been a pair of scholars to match Pizzigoni's and Townsend's combined grasp of colonial-era Nahuatl and skill as professional historians; this series is now adorned with their unique insights.

—Matthew Restall

In the 1970s James Lockhart, a young historian of early Latin America, made it his mission to travel through Mexico, seeking colonial-era documents written by indigenous people in their own languages. He was particularly interested in texts written in Nahuatl, the language spoken by the Nahuas of central Mexico, which he was in the midst of studying intensely. In the archive of Mexico's greatest museum, the Museo Nacional de Antropología, he came across the papers of a Native American family from the Toluca Valley. At the time relatively little was known about how the descendants of the people erroneously called "Aztecs" had actually spent their lives in the generations after contact. In an era before personal computers, Lockhart transcribed in longhand large chunks of Nahuatl text, underlining terms that were not yet familiar to him and marking the places he did not yet fully understand with question marks. Over time the De la Cruz family papers became one of the puzzle pieces he would fit together to write his magnum opus, *The Nahuas After the Conquest* (1992).

To finish *The Nahuas* Lockhart set aside the De la Cruz family papers, still only partially translated and studied to the extent pertinent to his book. It was years later, in 2001, when he passed the papers on to Caterina Pizzigoni to be used in her work on the Toluca Valley. Meanwhile, Pizzigoni had found other De la Cruz family papers (wills) in different archives in the course of her own work. For a long time the documents came up in conversation between them, with the hope of one day translating them fully and publishing them. Then Jim died suddenly in January 2014. A year later Caterina consulted with Camilla Townsend about certain elements of the papers, to find out that Camilla had been wondering about this very collection, as Jim had mentioned it to her.

It seemed the De la Cruz family papers were clearly meant to be transcribed, translated, and published, and we decided to do so for the papers' intrinsic value, as well as for the insight they offer into a great historian's work. This is our way of saying thank you for all that we learned from Jim in years of shared work, a small tribute to an unparalleled scholar and mentor. He believed deeply in letting the Nahuas speak for themselves in venues that reached the wider world, and thus we hope he would have been pleased with this book.

—Caterina Pizzigoni and Camilla Townsend

ACKNOWLEDGMENTS

This book is dedicated to James Lockhart, but numerous others helped us along the way. First and foremost, we wish to thank Stephanie Wood, *inhueltiuh*. She is the Elder Sister of the field of Nahuatl studies in the United States, not necessarily in years but certainly in a figurative sense. In the case of this book, she was invaluable, for her knowledge of Toluca is prodigious, her counsel always wise.

In Mexico we wish to thank the Instituto Nacional de Antropología e Historia and especially the director, Diego Prieto, for caring for the main documents and permitting us to publish them. We are grateful to historian María Teresa Jarquín Ortega, who pointed us to the Archivo Parroquial de San Pedro y San Pablo de Calimaya, and to Sergio Casas Candarabe, who helped us with research there. Julio César Gómez Hernández guided us on our visit to the old Franciscan church in Calimaya; he has lived its history and knows it well. We are also grateful to the staff of the Archivo General de la Nación in Mexico City, guardian of numerous relevant documents, including the wills of the book's protagonists; and to Daniel Rivera Rodríguez, who helped us collect needed documents when we ourselves were far away. In the fall of 2017, Lidia Gómez García (Benemérita Universidad Autónoma de Puebla) and Miguel Angel Ruz Barrio (Colegio Mexiquense, Toluca) invited us to present this project at their conference, "Fuentes y temas de etnohistoria mexicana." We profusely thank them and our many talented interlocutors at the gathering.

At Penn State University Press, we wish to thank Eleanor Goodman, executive editor; Matthew Restall, editor of the fantastic Latin American Originals series, which we are honored to be a part of; the invariably helpful staff at the press; our wonderful copyeditor, Susan Silver; and, last but not least, the two anonymous readers of the manuscript, who gave us inordinately useful feedback. We would also like to thank Columbia University and the Rutgers University School of Arts and Sciences Research Council for providing small subventions to help keep the purchase price down.

Gergely Baics turned out to be a mapmaker extraordinaire. We are forever in his debt!

Camilla wishes to thank John, Loren, and Cian for enriching her life, and Caterina is very grateful to Gergo, Emma, and Daria for their love and patience when she was working on this project.

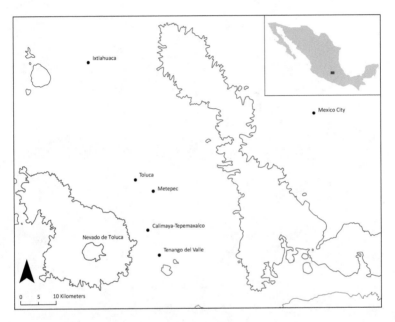

MAP 1 The Toluca Valley. Map by Gergely Baics.

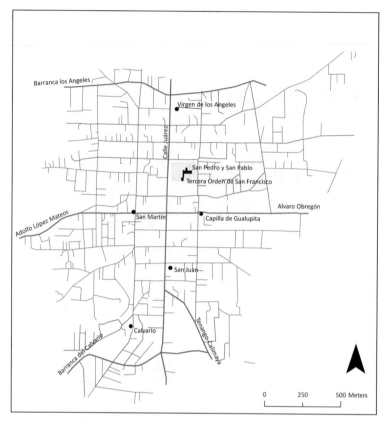

MAP 2 Calimaya with main streets and churches. Map by Gergely Baics.

Introduction

One October day in 1658, there was a great communal gathering at a field near the chapel of San Francisco in the indigenous town of Tepemaxalco, near Toluca. The people were there to plow and plant a new field, the products of which would be used to pay for improvements to the little church. There was a new head of the indigenous council that year. He was the one who orchestrated the event, and apparently some people were complaining about the trouble to which he was putting them all. "Perhaps it will be wondered at that the tribute field here at San Francisco was plowed," the new governor wrote in a record book he was keeping. "It was my yoke of oxen and my say-so. A few working men tilled the land and placed maguey plants belonging to them. Four of the rows of magueys are my property, and I placed them there, don Pedro de la Cruz, gobernador." Don Pedro was very insistent on the question of who was giving what. "People are never to say that perhaps they [the maguey plants] are the property of the whole altepetl. I sorted out the question of whose property they are. People were brought to swear." Don Pedro gave a long list of witnesses and then said, "Before all the witnesses of the working men and the women it was written down on this paper."[1]

That fleeting moment in time crystallized a great deal. On one level don Pedro had moved far from the world of his precolonial ancestors. He was writing in the Latin alphabet on a type of paper that his ancestors had never known, and he was recording what was

1. Instituto Nacional de Antropología e Historia, Mexico City, Biblioteca Nacional de Antropología e Historia, Archivo Histórico, Gómez Orozco 186.

being done to maintain a Christian chapel. Yet on another level he was merely marking and sealing the same kind of public agreement about land, agricultural tribute payments, and cooperative ventures that his people had been making time out of mind. In the old days, before the Spaniards came, the people would have come together to make public speeches about the communal arrangements they were making, and then a painter or scribe called a *tlacuilo* would have recorded the event by drawing certain glyphs on paper made of the maguey plant. Then the record would have been placed carefully in a reed basket kept by the chief. This time the written words reflecting the public pronouncements were deposited in a wooden box guarded by the indigenous governor. Don Pedro had been born about a hundred years after the Spaniards arrived. His grandparents' parents had been alive at the time the Europeans came. They might have been interested to see how closely their great-grandson's life resembled their own.

Attaining a realistic understanding of the effects of conquest has proven to be problematic. Paradoxical as it may sound, everything changed for the indigenous people, and at the same time nothing changed. On the one hand, the Spaniards achieved great power over many thousands of people, demanding regular payments of tribute, or tax, and insisting on the practice of their own religion of Christianity. Yet this extractive economy and Christian polity depended for its very existence on a kind of stability within the indigenous world at the level of the town, which the indigenous continued to call, in the language they continued to speak, the *altepetl* (meaning "water-mountain," because their ancient ancestors needed a water source and a defensible position). People do not entirely change the way they see the world or themselves overnight, or even from one decade to the next, and the Nahuas were no exception to this general principle.

It has been difficult for historians to determine what exactly indigenous peoples were thinking as the generations progressed, largely because they left few records revealing their own perspectives. After the Nahuas learned the Latin alphabet, they used it to write a great deal, but most of their writings were produced working in tandem with Spaniards or in response to Spanish legal demands and thus are of limited value in helping us to understand their more private worlds. Most of the preserved De la Cruz family papers, however, were written by Nahuas, for Nahuas, in response to pressing indigenous issues. They are thus inordinately valuable. They do not reveal explicit internal musings or obvious emotions, the way European letters or diaries would. The Nahuas had no experience with that sort of genre and were hardly disposed to open themselves up more than usual in the wake of conquest. But the records the De la Cruz family produced, intended to function as a communal memory, do reveal more private thoughts than we might at first expect. In them we see a family at work over the course of generations, men and women, old and young. We see not only what they spent their time doing but also what they worried about, what they grew angry about, and even what moved them in church. In short, they offer a rare vision of what had and had not changed after a century of life with Europeans.

In this book a sampling of the De la Cruz family papers has been translated into English. In setting forth the most important element of the collection, the family's primary record book, begun by don Pedro, we have elected to present the original language as well. There readers will see Indians writing in their own language of Nahuatl, and then gradually, over the course of time, switching into Spanish. Readers will be able to observe generational change with their own eyes, even as the tenor of the writing remains, to a large extent, profoundly consistent with the past.

The Toluca Valley

The Toluca Valley lies just west of the Valley of Mexico, separated by a high range of mountains. It was originally populated not by Nahuas but rather by the Matlatzinca, an indigenous culture group belonging to the Otomanguean-language family. A group of Nahuas called the Mexica (Me-SHEE-ka, the people known to us today as the "Aztecs"), together with their allies, invaded and conquered the region in the 1470s. After that, groups of Nahua colonizers from the central valley came to settle over the ensuing decades, and Nahuatl became the lingua franca. In the southern part of the valley, near a well-populated community called Calimaya, the Mexica seem to have established the much smaller altepetl of Tepemaxalco as a way of governing the locals. The Nahuatl names of some of Tepemaxalco's neighborhoods (or *tlaxilacalli*) reveal the types of migrants who arrived: "Place of the Temple Lords," "Place of the Rulers," "Place of the Merchants," and "Place of the Mexica People." The new arrangements apparently generated a certain degree of ethnic conflict; some level of resentment would percolate through future generations. The De la Cruz family lived in Tepemaxalco, and they still distrusted people from Calimaya.[2]

The Spaniards first arrived during the period of the conquest of Mexico-Tenochtitlan (1519–21) and shortly afterward established four administrative town centers: Ixtlahuaca, Toluca, Metepec, and Tenango del Valle (see map 1). The boundaries of these jurisdictions changed over time, and Toluca and its surroundings became part of the Marquesado del Valle, originally given to Hernando Cortés. Metepec and the nearby towns of Calimaya and Tepemaxalco—taken together, one of the most extended, populated, and wealthy concessions of the valley—were given in *encomienda* as a labor grant to Juan Gutiérrez Altamirano, a relative of Cortés. The surname "Altamirano" was adopted shortly thereafter by some leading indigenous inhabitants of Tepemaxalco.[3]

When the Spaniards came across the closely linked Calimaya and Tepemaxalco, they institutionalized a double altepetl: the two entities shared the same parish church and a pair of patron saints who gave them their Christian names: San Pedro for Calimaya and San Pablo for Tepemaxalco. However, they maintained separate governors (*gobernadores*) and town councils (*cabildos*), as well as distinct sets of tlaxilacalli. The eight tlaxilacalli of Tepemaxalco are known precisely through the tribute lists preserved by the De la Cruz family: Teocaltitlan Tlatocapan (or Teopanquiyahuac), Pasiontitlan, San Francisco Pochtlan, Tlatocapan, Mexicapan, San Lucas Evangelista, Santa María de la Asunción, and Santiago.[4] In 1558 the Spanish authorities ordered the congregation of Calimaya and Tepemaxalco

---

2. García Castro, *Indios, territorio, y poder*, 44–50, 57–61, 114, 394–95. See also Hernández Rodríguez, "Historia prehispanica," in Rosenzweig et al., *Breve historia*, 19–62, and Gerhard, *Guide to the Historical Geography*, 174–78, 270–73, 330–31.

3. Hernández Rodríguez, "Conquista española," and Jarquín Ortega, "Formación de una nueva sociedad," both in Rosenzweig et al., *Breve historia*, 65–76, 77–139; García Castro, *Indios, territorio, y poder*, 106–7, 114, 117–20. On the history of the Toluca Valley, see Wood, "Corporate Adjustments."

4. The reconstruction of the tlaxilacalli of Tepemaxalco comes from Pizzigoni, *Testaments of Toluca*. In the same book we also find those of Calimaya, although we know fewer of them and we do not know the order: Pasiontitlan, Tlamimilolpan, Teopantonco, Teopanquiyahuac, and San Antonio de Padua.

into one urban center, tying them together even further, although the two would remain separate barrios, with independent governments, saints, and jurisdictions.[5]

As in the rest of the valley, Tepemaxalco's economy was based essentially on the cultivation of maize, favored by the altitude and cool climate. Livestock raising was also important. Besides being essential for local consumption, maize and other agricultural products largely fed the market of Mexico City and, to a lesser extent, the mining centers in the southwest: Zultepec and Tematzcaltepec. The indigenous communities also sent their tribute in the same direction.

The colonial authorities were present in Toluca through a *corregidor* (district administrative officer), and in Metepec and Tenango del Valle with *alcaldes mayores* (more powerful regional administrative officers). Tepemaxalco was placed under the alcalde mayor of Metepec. As for the Spanish population more broadly, the *encomenderos*, or recipients of *encomiendas*, were largely absent, living mainly in Mexico City. They and their families had been linked to Hernando Cortés and his closest associates and were now among the colony's most elite individuals. The Spaniards who actually lived in the valley were substantially smaller and relatively poorer farmers, living on the property of grander men or in indigenous villages nearby. At times they ran sweatshops or tanneries or acted as muleteers and small merchants, moving goods to Mexico City.

As for the church, the Franciscans arrived in the town of Toluca first, establishing their main church in 1529–30 and a *convento*, a religious house, with four friars. They also founded conventos in Jilotepec (1530), Calimaya (1557), Metepec (around 1569), and Zinacantepec (1569), with just two friars each. Between 1537 and 1543 the Augustinians established themselves in Toluca as well as at Ocuilan and Malinalco; later they were also present in Capulhuac, Tianguistenco, and Zacualpan. Much later in the seventeenth century came the discalced Carmelites, the Mercedarians, and the hospital order of San Juan de Dios, who all built their homes in Toluca. The secular clergy arrived around 1535 and were much more dispersed

---

5. Jarquín Ortega, "Formación de una nueva sociedad," in Rosenzweig et al., *Breve historia*, 111–16, 124–26; Gerhard, *Guide to the Historical Geography*; García Castro, *Indios, territorio, y poder*, 145–53, 160–61, 438. See also Loera y Chávez de Esteinou, *Calimaya y Tepemaxalco*.

through the countryside, usually with one representative in a given town, often sent by *encomendero* families residing in Mexico City. Through the process of secularization, the secular church gradually replaced friars as heads of parishes, but the situation was always mixed in the valley, and this process did not become truly advanced until a relatively late date; in fact, it was only around 1756 that most friaries passed under the control of the secular clergy.[6]

Overall, the Spanish presence was limited to the main town centers, while the countryside remained quintessentially indigenous all through the seventeenth century. True, Spanish priests as well as small farmers, traders, and modest business owners, often with ties to Mexico City, started to live in proximity to indigenous communities and became the main vehicle for social and cultural change. But the rural areas remained, in effect, a kind of "Indian Country." Thus Tepe-maxalco, at the time of Pedro de la Cruz and later, was an indigenous altepetl run by indigenous officials, with a couple of Franciscan friars nearby in Calimaya and a priest and/or an alcalde mayor who visited every now and then. The documents of the De la Cruz family reveal fascinating aspects of life in Tepemaxalco.[7] The people went about their business in their lovely valley, ever conscious of the looming Nevado de Toluca, their imposing snow-capped mountain, which had stood at the edge of their world time out of mind. Some elements of their lives had changed profoundly; others, however, had not.

Characteristics of the Documents

Today the most important family papers of don Pedro de la Cruz and his descendants are preserved in the archive of the Museo Nacional de Antropología in Mexico City. These consist of a pair of books, numbers 185 and 186 of the Gómez Orozco collection. The first is a tribute roll book maintained by don Pedro de la Cruz from 1657

6. See Jarquín Ortega, "Formación de una nueva sociedad," in Rosenzweig et al., *Breve historia,* 91–98, 122–23; Gerhard, *Guide to the Historical Geography,* 330–31; and Borges, *Religiosos en Hispanoamérica,* 22–23, 203–5, 221–23.

7. Lockhart, *Nahuas After the Conquest,* has details about the protagonists of these papers, the De la Cruz family (see especially 136–38 and 230–35). Lockhart studied the Toluca Valley quite closely in the chapter "Spaniards Among Indians," 202–41, and also in "Capital and Province," in Altman and Lockhart, *Provinces of Early Mexico,* 99–123.

to 1665, the first eight years of his governorship. He kept two types of records in the book. First, every year he copied out the names of each head of family presently living in each of the eight tlaxilacalli of Tepemaxalco (see document 2). Every adult owed three *tostones* (or 1.5 pesos) per year. Thus, married male heads of family owed six tostones, and widows or widowers owed three. Single adult men were also listed as owing three; there were few of these. Only the very rarest of single adult women lived on their own. Nobles were by no means excluded, but they paid no more than anybody else. In another part of the book, don Pedro made an entry every time someone came to pay tribute money over the course of the year. These were elected officials who bore the contributions of multiple people. Don Pedro would write out in words the amount being turned over to him, and then, given the largely illiterate population, he would draw a picture of the proper number of one-peso coins, half-peso tostones, and the smaller coins representing *reales* (worth one-eighth of a peso each) or *cuartillos* (one-quarter each) so that the person depositing money could be absolutely sure that the full amount was recorded (see document 2, deposits from 1658).

The second book was something altogether different, unique to the De la Cruz family (see document 1). Don Pedro began the book in 1647 to document contributions to local churches with which he was involved. At the time, he was collecting large amounts of money from the leading families in the area so that they could buy an organ for 400 pesos. He did not mention which church the organ was for. He was *mayordomo*, or steward, of the church of San Francisco in the tlaxilacalli of Pochtlan but also heavily involved in a chapel dedicated to San Juan, his father's name saint; in addition, in 1647 the church of the tlaxilacalli of Santa María de la Asunción, which was near his main residence, was undergoing renovations, so he could have meant that one (see map 2 for the churches). For a decade don Pedro desultorily kept the book as a record of various church expenses and of the ways that any needed funds had been raised. Then, in 1656, a great crisis exploded around him, in which a significant part of the population of Calimaya-Tepemaxalco decided to protest the tribute system and slipped away when it was to be collected.[8] In 1657 don Pedro was

8. Archivo General de la Nación (hereafter cited as AGN), Mexico City, Indios, vol. 18, exp. 222, 1655, "Para que el alcalde mayor de Metepec no cobre de los naturales de Tepemajalco mas servicio real del que deben pagar en cada año, recibiendoles en

elected *gobernador* of the altepetl of Tepemaxalco. He apparently was to be the one to find a way to maintain peace. He took this larger role very seriously, and the next year the nature of the book changed.

Somewhere—perhaps on a trip to Mexico City, perhaps during a visit to an older relative —don Pedro had apparently seen a traditional set of Nahua historical annals. The *xiuhpohualli* (or year count) had long been part of Mesoamerican life; for generations, a long strip of calendrical dates paired with glyphs acting as mnemonic devices had inspired trained reciters to give performances of a people's history. A modernized version of the *xiuhpohualli* had taken on new life in the sixteenth century: students of the friars who had learned the Latin alphabet began to transcribe historical performances, or parts of performances, by their elders. Those written texts then circulated among indigenous intellectuals for generations, changing over the years as they were copied, abstracted, or expanded. After a symbol or notation for a given year, the writer would follow with events of interest to the entire altepetl—the governorship and other rotating offices on the indigenous cabildo, major meteorological phenomena, droughts, epidemics, and so on.[9]

In 1658 don Pedro, in writing his book of records, suddenly dropped back to 1607, when a once-renowned gobernador was

cuenta lo que tienen pagado según la certificación del contador de tributos" [Petition that the alcalde mayor of Metepec not demand from the natives of Tepemaxalco more tribute than that which they are bound to pay each year, receiving it in the account that they have fully paid, according to a certificate from the tribute accountant]; AGN, Indios, vol. 20, exp. 61, 1656, "Para que el alcalde mayor de Metepec guarde y cumpla el mandamiento de gobierno despachado al gobernador y alcaldes del pueblo de Calimaya y Tepemachalco para que no les cobre mas cantidad de lo que deben pagar al año de servicio real" [Petition that the alcalde mayor of Metepec keep and abide by the order sent to the governor and cabildo members of the (joint) town of Calimaya-and-Tepemaxalco, so that he not charge them more than the annual required tribute]. See also a later document: AGN, Indios, vol. 24, exp. 25, 1666, "Su excelencia manda a las justicias, gobernadores, y otros ministros de los partidos donde estuvieren indios que se hubieren ausentado del pueblo de Tepemajalco de la jurisdicción de Metepec y sus sujetos matriculados en ellos en la ultima tasación, den al gobernador y oficiales de república todo el favor y ayuda para cobrar a los naturales los tributos que están debiendo" [His Excellency commands that the judges, governors, and other ministers of the districts where the Indians were who had absented themselves from the town of Tepemaxalco, of the Metepec jurisdiction, and were its matriculated subjects at the time of the last taxation, give to the governor and officials of the republic all help and aid in order to receive from the natives the tribute payments that are still outstanding].

9. For the most recent study of the genre, see Townsend, *Annals of Native America*.

remembered to have died, and then he proceeded through the seventeenth century in true annals style, soon covering the 1640s and 1650s again, this time offering more than a record of a particular church's fund-raising efforts. Yet don Pedro was at heart an accountant, and the financial aspects of his community's experience continued to dominate his history even when he started to write about other arenas. In 1659 he began, for example, "Now on Friday, the 3rd of January, at four o'clock, there was a strong earthquake at the time of the [installation] ceremonies for don Pedro de la Cruz, gobernador. On Saturday, the 4th of January, there was another earthquake at one o'clock." But then suddenly don Pedro abruptly changed direction: "In the year 1659, I had been keeping the money of the *cantores* [church musicians] so that they could cover the cost of some trumpets and a guitar and a rebeck. All the money was spent. There is no more left of what I was keeping from the corn harvested in 1657, for which they got seven reales per fanega." In general, although the form of the book is that of a set of annals, with elegant, darkened writing marking the start of each new year, the substance of most of its content remains the community's finances.

Yet the De la Cruz family did understand the book to constitute a set of traditional annals, for the work continued past the life and work of one man, as annals (but not account books) were always intended to do. When don Pedro died, his son-in-law, together with his daughter, continued to maintain the book, and on their watch material more typical of the annals was included, along with financial accounts. In the eighteenth century a De la Cruz who was probably the latter couple's grandson took over the book, and after him came five more generations of interested family members. By the end—the last entry is dated 1842—the writers had largely lost sight of what kind of material would have been included by their ancestors, but they added entries nonetheless. They explicitly connected themselves to the past, and implicitly to the future, just as any reciter of a *xiuh-pohualli* would have done in the early sixteenth century.

The book also resembles ancient annals in that it is not a bound set of original legal records but rather consists of each writer's compendium of events. When don Pedro states, for example, "Here we place our signatures," he then signs all the witnesses' names himself, in his own handwriting. We are not seeing the original documentation of the land transfer or will or receipt for cash but rather don

Pedro's copy of what he deems important enough to include. Significantly, we can also see each generation's exact contribution to the volume. The handwriting and style alter notably with each generational changing of the guard; this is not a later copy prepared by one interested descendant in a seamless text, as we often find is the case for surviving annals. It is very clearly an original family record book maintained over multiple generations. Very possibly, more such family records will emerge in the future from local, village-level archives. Other scholars have already noted that the papers of local indigenous church officials sometimes bear a resemblance to the De la Cruz family papers.[10] In the meantime, however, the book kept by don Pedro de la Cruz and his descendants is uniquely interesting.

In addition, much of his personality and life breathes through his last will and testament, as well as the testament of his son-in-law, don Juan, so the two documents are also presented here. Other aspects of their lives are revealed in the local church's baptismal records, kept in Nahuatl by Nahuas and only occasionally glanced at by a priest. These documents, together with the two family record books, bring the picture of don Pedro, his descendants, and the community of Tepemaxalco into focus and speak to us even today.

A careful reader can learn about life in a particular family; about community relations writ somewhat larger (including potential tensions around class, gender, and ethnicity); about the altepetl's interactions with the wider Spanish world; and even about notions of the divine. At no point is any writer in the volume obviously introspective or grandly philosophical, but listening carefully to every word nevertheless turns out to be profoundly illuminating.

The De la Cruz Family

The status of the De la Cruz family seems to have risen in the midst of the changes brought about in the Toluca Valley after the conquest. There is no evidence that the family had any sense of themselves as being descended from an important or ancient noble line; they were very interested in history and undoubtedly would have mentioned it if they had harbored such a belief. (After ten years in office as

---

10. Gómez García, *Anales nahuas*.

the governor, don Pedro did once refer to himself as the *tlatoani*, or ruler; that was as close as he ever came to using the ancient language pertaining to nobility in reference to himself.) Spanish records tell us that there was a Pedro de la Cruz from the region of Calimaya who became a successful muleteer in the late sixteenth century—an occupation open to leading indigenous citizens (unlike the professions, which explicitly excluded them). This man most likely launched the clan of successful De la Cruzes we find in the seventeenth century.[11] They held scattered lands, which had been typical of the rich before the conquest and continued so afterward. The wealthy don Diego de la Cruz, who lived in Tlatocapan, the leading or first-listed tlaxilacalli of Tepemaxalco, became the first De la Cruz to be elected governor in 1655, shortly before don Pedro did in 1657. Don Pedro was probably don Diego's nephew or else a cousin; he was not his son. Pedro and his family lived not in the leading neighborhood but in the tlaxilacalli of Pasiontitlan. Pedro's father, Juan de la Cruz, never became governor, though he did serve on the cabildo. In addition to extensive lands, Juan and his son possessed large numbers of oxen and mules, surely tying them to the Pedro de la Cruz who ran the original mule-train business.[12]

When don Pedro became governor in 1657, he would have been at least thirty, as it was not a position accorded the very young except in emergencies caused by demographic disaster. He was thus born no later than the 1620s: no wonder the detailed and even personal memories included in the annals section begin in the mid-1630s. For instance, when a great snow came on February 24, 1635, we are told that it was the day of San Matías, or Saint Matthias, the Apostle. The next year a little bridge had to be replaced. The villagers pushed the old one out into the water from the side where the church of San Francisco was, then set it ablaze. During the exciting years of his youth, don Pedro was receiving a Spanish-style education, probably

11. Lockhart, *Nahuas After the Conquest*, 136–38. García Castro notes the general pattern of old noble families falling into hard times and other elites rising to take their places after about 1580 (*Indios, territorio, y poder*, 172–83).

12. See the testaments of don Pedro de la Cruz and don Juan de la Cruz, included here as documents 4 and 5. The people residing in each tlaxilacalli are listed in the De la Cruz family volume delineating tribute payments (document 2). For treatment of the family through the years, see Pizzigoni, *Life Within*, 213–16. García Castro also has don Diego and don Pedro in his list of governors of Tepemaxalco (*Indios, territorio, y poder*, 417–18).

from the Franciscans of the convento of San Pedro and San Pablo in Calimaya, though conceivably from another educated Nahua. He learned to write in a fine, decorative hand. Nor was he alone in his studies: most of his peers—boys from other upper-level indigenous families—learned to sign their names with flourishes, to play various instruments, and to sing. Indeed, the sons of the leading families were often referred to as cantores in his writings, and, as musicians, they worked together not only to buy fine instruments for various local churches but also to keep the houses of worship in good repair. Don Pedro, who played the organ, truly loved music and was knowledgeable about it, once even ordering from Mexico City the score of a *villancico* (a sort of folk song) dedicated to San Pedro (his namesake saint).

When don Pedro was elected governor, he took on all the activities typical of the office. Not only did he chair cabildo meetings and collect and deliver the required tribute, but he also continued to take an active role in more enjoyable aspects of community affairs. Mostly, this meant that he continued to raise money for church improvements and for festival days and processions and took charge of buying what was needed for all of these. He also participated in public ceremonies commemorating land transfers. Indeed, it was in regard to one of the latter that he displayed a rare fit of pique. He and an entourage of relevant cabildo members had gone to the tlaxilacalli of San Lucas one Friday evening in 1660 for an event, and they were deluged with rain inside the church, the thatch roof apparently having thinned and rotted in places, as thatch often did. He had with him a large cloak, probably intended for use in the ceremony, and they used it as a sort of canopy to block the rain. "No one took care of it until Monday, when the gobernador himself removed it and spread it outside [to dry]." Most unluckily, a roaming band of pigs mauled it ("ate it up on him") so that the event's total cost to him personally, he complained, was "sixteen pesos, one real, plus one of his cloaks."

Perhaps most important to don Pedro was the role he played in regard to preserving his people's culture. Not only did he see to it that they held their own in the world of Spanish-style church art and music, but he also maintained what he clearly perceived to be a traditional book of both history (the segment of Nahuatl annals of the past) and history in the making (the record of public events that together composed the life of the altepetl). In this regard, he shared his sense of what an elite indigenous man owed to posterity with contemporary Nahua nobles elsewhere in Mexico.[13] History keeping had been one of the traditional duties of the indigenous elite since long before the conquest, and don Pedro, like others, seems to have been aware of this fact.

By the early 1660s, don Pedro's children were growing up (see figure 1). His wife, Ana Juana, was the daughter of Sebastián Jacobo of Tlatocapan, who sometimes served as a cabildo member.[14] Pedro and Ana Juana had raised a daughter, Josepha Francisca, probably named for don Pedro's mother. She now married a local boy named Juan, who then took his wife's prestigious "de la Cruz" surname. Juan's father, Nicolás Gaspar, was a neighbor in Pasiontitlan; he was not a cabildo member at that time, but Juan's mother was María de la Cruz, almost certainly kin.[15] In 1662 Juan himself was listed for the first time as a tribute-paying householder in the tlaxilacalli, so he and Josepha probably were married in that year or not too long before. Decades later Juan would give Josepha Francisca credit for having arranged their children's marriages. Had her own marriage likewise been arranged according to custom? Yes, don Juan even mentions in his will that his marriage had been arranged. But don Pedro and Ana Juana may well have made an arrangement to suit their daughter. The fact that the groom was a well-known neighbor whose father was not elite enough to have served on the cabildo indicates that Josepha Francisca likely had at least some choice in the matter. Over the years she would prove herself to be an active participant in her marriage and in the community, even adding notations to the book of history, albeit through a scribe.[16]

Meanwhile, it seems that don Pedro had other children out of wedlock. Such a step would have been entirely consistent with

13. See Zapata y Mendoza, *Historia cronológica*.
14. Based on the year in which her own daughter married, we can say that Ana Juana was probably born around 1635. The surviving birth records of her family's church begin in 1638, and, sure enough, in the late 1630s and early 1640s, we find several younger siblings born to her father, Sebastián Jacobo, and her mother, Ana Mónica. Archivo Parroquial de San Pedro y San Pablo de Calimaya, Bautizos 001, 1634–55.
15. The births of children to Nicolás Gaspar and María de la Cruz are recorded regularly throughout the 1640s. Archivo Parroquial, Bautizos 001, 1634–55.
16. Testament of don Juan de la Cruz, document 5, in combination with the De la Cruz family papers.

ancient Nahua practice; in the old days noblemen always had multiple wives. In the parish record of baptisms, someone named Pedro de la Cruz is occasionally listed as "father." There could have been another man of that name, but one young woman, also named Josepha, was recognized as a sister by don Pedro's legitimate daughter; she even arranged a marriage for her, according to her husband's will. And one young man, Felipe de la Cruz, she referred to as a brother. Felipe began to work as a scribe in the 1660s and may even have helped his father write out parts of his book, given slight variations in the handwriting seen there. He took down his father's will in 1667, when don Pedro had a scare and thought he was going to die; Felipe himself received nothing in the will, but he would have understood that. It wasn't just a Christian practice. In preconquest days, as well, only a nobleman's children by certain wives expected to inherit. Pedro's and Ana Juana's legitimate daughter, Josepha Francisca, and the three children she had given birth to by then were to have received everything.[17]

Between 1657 and the late 1670s, don Pedro continued to serve as governor, with two brief interruptions, one of six months and one of a year, both probably due to illness. Generally, in the Nahua world, office rotated regularly. Other governors of Tepemaxalco had, however, likewise served stints longer than a year or two: one even seems to have served for thirty years.[18] Don Pedro was a well-known citizen who often served as a godfather when his friends and relations had children.[19] Probably at least part of the reason don Pedro was able to hold onto power for so long lay in the fact that he regularly gave enormous donations toward community debts and projects. In 1666, for instance, besides being involved in resolving another crisis around some commoners' nonpayment of tribute, he also donated 400 pesos to buy another organ, this time for the main church of San Pedro y San Pablo (see map 2).[20] But, despite his many activities, death did eventually catch up with him. In 1674 he petitioned for formal permission to establish a chapel he had been working on for years,

17. Testament of don Pedro de la Cruz, document 4.
18. The other notable case was don Baltazar de los Reyes, who was governor of Tepemaxalco from 1624 to 1654 (see García Castro, *Indios, territorio, y poder*, 417–18).
19. There are several references to Don Pedro acting as a godfather in the Nahuatl records of the Archivo Parroquial, Bautizos 001, 1634–55.
20. See AGN, "Su excelencia manda."

dedicated to the Virgin of Guadalupe, and that same year he stopped writing in his book.[21] He breathed his last somewhere between that point and September 1678, when another man, don Juan Martín, was explicitly mentioned as being governor (and don Pedro's son-in-law had taken over the book).

The preceding year had been a dreadful one for the family. In June 1677, when don Pedro's son-in-law, don Juan, was celebrating the festival of his name-day saint, he was attacked and beaten by a group of men. Had he angered someone? Or was he simply a tipsy man with a full purse? He did not say. In either case the sight of him after the beating apparently triggered a stroke in his mother-in-law, don Pedro's widow, doña Ana Juana. We are told only that her problems began then, that she was still and silent for a week and then died. Don Juan would always remember his wife working to prepare her mother for burial and then watching her be placed in the ground. Don Juan soon traveled to Toluca to file charges against his attackers and receive medical attention. He remained there for a long time, first growing worse but eventually better. While he was away, the smallpox epidemic that was beginning that year apparently struck Tepemaxalco. He does not say so exactly, but simply that before he could return, Josepha's brother Felipe died, as did his sister Catarina and another brother-in-law, as well as his beloved mother, María. The family—undoubtedly the whole town—had been decimated. "It all happened in that same year," he said tersely, trying to come to terms with the rapidity of such calamitous erasure without succumbing to self-pity. He struggled against oblivion. "Here let it be known," he wrote. (The sentiment was a typical refrain in the book, but here the words took a form different from the ubiquitous "here it will appear," with which he paired the phrase.)

When it seemed matters couldn't be worse, an old friend, don Lorenzo López, who had served on the cabildo with don Juan, was for

21. AGN, Indios, vol. 25, exp. 19, 1674, "Que el alcalde mayor de este pueblo de la jurisdicción de Metepec y el padre ministro de doctrina informe del caudal de don Pedro de la Cruz, gobernador del mismo pueblo para poder resolver sobre la licencia que pide para fundar una hermita a la santísima Virgen de Guadalupe" [An order that the alcalde mayor of this pueblo in the jurisdiction of Metepec, and the priest who ministers to the parish, investigate the wealth of don Pedro de la Cruz, governor of the same pueblo, in order to resolve the question of giving him the permission he requests to found a chapel dedicated to the most holy Virgin of Guadalupe]. Earlier, he referred to his project in his 1667 will.

some reason arrested by an alcalde from the more powerful town of Calimaya (a man named Francisco de la Cruz, ironically) and imprisoned in Metepec; the alcalde named Francisco continued "speaking calumnies." Don Juan chose to ask the Franciscan *guardián* (head of the convento) to intervene; the friar would have known don Lorenzo personally, as he had recently served as the *maestro de capilla* (choir master) of the town's main church. We cannot know what the argument was about, but don Lorenzo was released and a year later again served as *maestro de capilla*.

In 1682 don Juan was elected governor and later that decade served for another three years. He pursued activities similar to those of his father-in-law, but he mentioned his wife far more often than don Pedro had ever mentioned his (although don Pedro certainly did respect his wife, leaving her as his executor). Indeed, in the new generation the book seemed to belong to both husband and wife, in that Josepha at one point even dictated an entry (about the death of her maternal grandfather, whom she herself shrouded, just as she did for her mother). By now it was the late seventeenth century, and Mexico was in full baroque swing. In 1683, under don Juan's leadership, the altepetl launched a lavish renovation of the main convento's church, even bringing in a Spanish craftsman and his assistants. Don Juan went to Mexico City to make the initial arrangements, and later, after the painters were installed in his home, doña Josepha sent another man back to the city to buy ingredients that it turned out she needed to prepare Spanish-style food for the guests—cinnamon, saffron, olives, olive oil, and so on.

Don Juan died in 1691—or at least his last will and testament is dated then. He was proud that he had done his duty as governor: "I did well in completing the quota of tribute collected." He owed nothing and forbade anyone from complaining, "for all the books are there in which are designated what was spent as expenses." His wife Josepha was already dead, but he left behind him five children by her—Jacinto, Josepha, Juana, Pedro, and María—all of whom were well provided for. He was also survived by a second wife, Melchora María, and several children by her. Don Juan's eldest son, Jacinto, died only two years after his father, without any surviving children, but years later, his wife, Polonia María, left almost everything to a nephew, Francisco Nicolás de la Cruz, who became governor in the

De la Cruz Family Tree

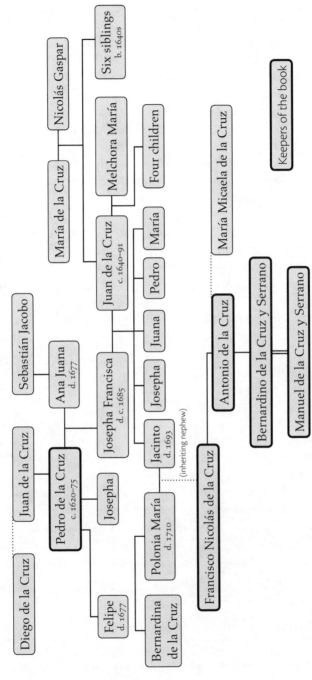

FIG. 1 De la Cruz family tree. Diagram by the authors.

1740s and added a bit to the book.[22] His nephew don Antonio de la Cruz served in the 1770s and likewise added a few notes. A son or nephew of Antonios, don Bernardino de la Cruz y Serrano (the Serranos were a long-standing indigenous line from the tlaxilacalli of Santiago) served in the 1790s and early 1800s. And a grandson of his, Manuel de la Cruz y Serrano, was still commenting in the margins and translating pieces from the Nahuatl into Spanish in the 1840s. The eighteenth-century don Bernardino referred to himself as a "descendant of the conquistador don Pedro de la Cruz y Serrano"—which showed a certain misunderstanding of the situation, but a misunderstanding mixed with a genuine family reverence for don Pedro with which the latter would certainly have been pleased. Nineteenth-century Manuel referred to don Nicolás de la Cruz as his grandfather's grandfather and proudly commented on his contributions to the commonwealth (see figure 1). The book had become a sort of family history—it was no longer a record of the entire altepetl—yet the family's engagement with the wider world was still what mattered to the writers. In the world they knew, the church bells that their family had long tended to the maintenance of, for instance, rang joyously and sometimes dolorously throughout the town, and they were glad of it.

Community Relations

In the late 1650s and early 1660s, there were approximately 185 heads of household recorded as tribute payers in don Pedro's roll book. The number varied slightly from year to year, as elders died and young people married and set up households. It is probably safe to use the typical multiplier of five to determine a rough population count of something like 1,000 people, of whom we can assume about half were males. In don Pedro's annals-style book, over the course of the 1650s and 1660s, he mentions slightly more than 50 individual indigenous men as officials on the cabildo or in one of the churches

---

22. The heir named Nicolás de la Cruz could conceivably have been the father of the Nicolás de la Cruz who began to write in the book, but the timing makes this unlikely. See testaments of don Juan de la Cruz (1691; document 5) here, as well as Jacinto de la Cruz (1693) and Polonia María (1710) in Pizzigoni, *Testaments of Toluca*.

or as possessors of obvious wealth or the title "don." Some of these were clearly related as fathers and sons or as brothers; they were not necessarily all heads of household. (His own son Felipe de la Cruz, for instance, was mentioned as a scribe when he was too young to have a house of his own, and in fact he tragically died young in the epidemic of 1677–78.) So it seems that in a particular decade, roughly 50 out of 500 men in the area were local notables, or what the Spaniards called *principales* in their documents. Scanning the list of householders in the account book produces a comparable result: approximately 1 out of 10 of them is recognizable as a sort of *principal* after reading don Pedro's annals-style book. The *pipiltin,* or nobles of the ancien régime, are also often thought to have constituted about 10 percent of the rural population.

The principales owned land and oxen. They were the ones elected to the cabildo, rotating the positions available among themselves over time. A number are mentioned as artisans and many as musicians. They were all educated to some extent in the Latin alphabet, as they could sign their names, and at least some of them could surely read the European musical scores don Pedro bought for them. Indeed, the cantores are occasionally referred to in the text as *teopantlaca* (church people), a term that at least in the sixteenth century definitely implied a church education. Although such men went to the fields on communal-labor draft days, when they were planting or harvesting lands whose produce was dedicated to a particular chapel or church, it is likely that they did so more as supervisors and organizers than as laborers; we cannot be sure of this, however. Some may well have been active farming men themselves.

Don Pedro regularly called the nonprincipales *tlapaliuque* (literally, "vigorous persons," but conveying the idea of working men). He used the term *macehualtin* (the old term for commoners, used in opposition to *pipiltin*) only a single time (though later in the century his son-in-law would use it more). So don Pedro thought and spoke of the common men around him as those who did physical labor. He tells us that they owned no oxen and could bring only their digging sticks to communal-labor projects. In a couple of cases, it is clear that an impoverished individual also owned no land, but most of the tlapaliuque did apparently have plots to call their own. In earlier times the *tlatoani* would have distributed communally held land to individual families who needed it; apparently those allotments, no matter how small, were now understood to be the private property of individual families.

In the families of the working men, women definitely pulled their weight. It has long been understood that Mesoamerican gender roles were complementary, almost never set up in competition with each other or with any sense of an adversarial relationship at home. Interestingly, this record teaches us that in public or communal-labor projects, it was likewise understood that men and women each had their appointed tasks. On the day in October 1658 with which this book opened, the working people present as witnesses were not only men but also women. The women's names were not all listed as the men's were—it is quite possible that don Pedro did not even know all their names—but he noted their leader: "The *cihuatepixqui* was Juana Hernández." A woman by that name is listed as a widow in the 1658 tribute notebook. The concept of a *cihuatepixqui* (literally "woman keeper or guardian of people") must have descended from an older era, for it certainly was not common in the rather patriarchal colonial era, and indeed, the term appears only rarely in the Nahuatl-language records produced under the auspices of the Spaniards. Interestingly, the working women may well have ceded authority most often to a woman from a relatively prominent family, for this Juana had a Spanish-style last name, not typical for most rural working peoples, and that particular last name was shared by two men who held cabildo posts in the early 1650s (Pedro and Francisco Hernández). The notion of relatively elite women leading the women just as elite men led the men could not have been utterly foreign in this region, for at one point, in 1683, don Juan de la Cruz referred to himself as "don Juan de la Cruz, gobernador, with doña Josepha Francisca, *gobernadora*." Gender parallelism may have run deep in some ways. In local wills testators, including don Pedro, often referred to their love and devotion of the "*santosme* and *santasme*" (literally "the male and female saints").

Everywhere we turn in the texts we seem to see evidence of the cooperation or reciprocity that remains a signal feature of Nahua village life to this day. Anthropologists have illuminated a world in which this cooperation is both voluntary and obligatory, as one's behavior in this regard forms the heart of one's reputation in the eyes of peers. A man who holds office has the responsibility not merely of contributing heavily to communal projects but also of motivating others to do likewise. His own reputation is at stake, but it is understood that his motivation for acting cannot merely be self-aggrandizement.[23]

Despite the picture we glimpse in the De la Cruz family papers of people working together, it is nevertheless undeniable that there were some visible tensions between the two social groups—the principales and the tlapaliuque. In his text don Pedro mentions constantly that he and his cohort are paying for everything, or nearly everything, or contributing most to a communal day of labor, thanks to their oxen; he equally regularly insists that the entire altepetl should not attempt to take credit for what he and a few other generous souls have done. One early comment in 1656 is emblematic of numerous others: "Concerning how the corncrib was built: People are never to say that perhaps the altepetl did it, for only we cantores bestirred ourselves. We built the corncrib. We spent two pesos, two reales, to pay the carpenters. . . . People are never to say that perhaps the working men did it, because they only helped thatch it, and only a few hauled wood."

It is impossible to believe that don Pedro would have harped so on this theme if there weren't at least occasional complaints on the part of working men that the principales did not do enough, but, when we consider the context, it becomes abundantly clear why don Pedro so constantly trumpeted his own role. He had become governor, we must remember, in the midst of a great tribute crisis, in which the people of Tepemaxalco were resisting payment. On the final pages of the tribute notebook, he recorded the fact that in that very year, he purchased 360 sheep for the community, presumably to help them pay their debt to the state. Looking at the annual records in that same notebook, we see that the people almost never managed to scrape together all that they owed. Presumably, don Pedro himself had to pay the difference; otherwise, he would have gone to prison (as indigenous noblemen elsewhere often did, for that very reason). In his will he is careful to explain that he does not owe any leftover tribute.

Don Pedro was nothing if not accurate; he did not always claim credit. At one point he specifically acknowledged that he had not paid

---

23. Magazine says succinctly, "We [in urban America] live together as subjects in a world of objects, while they [in Nahua village life] live in a world of persons, mediated by objects" (*Village Is Like a Wheel*, 5).

for everything: "We bought three granaries, their price twelve pesos and two reales. The money came from the little tribute field San Juan has at Pelaxtitlan. And one corncrib was purchased by Sr. don Pedro de la Cruz, gobernador. It is his property. People are never to say that maybe all three are his property." He even sometimes implicitly criticized his children for being grudging toward the working people. "Don Pedro de la Cruz gave 120 pesos to [the church of] Santa María de la Asunción. People are not to get upset. His children and grand-children are not to dishonor the agreement." Years later his son-in-law don Juan would similarly warn his own son not to try to get back property the family had gifted to cousins.[24] These perorations are very much in keeping with some mid-sixteenth-century docu-ments from Tetzcoco, in which living people argue about the nature of a gift made by a long-dead figure, and hostility to commoners had absolutely nothing to do with it.[25] So most likely don Pedro's style is as revealing of a cultural desire to render communal contribution matters completely clear as of a need to argue with potentially critical or complaining tlapaliuque.

Some might want to read don Pedro's defensiveness as a desire to cover up his own abuse of the less fortunate or even theft, on his part, of communal monies; certainly our modern interests in class tensions and corruption prompt us to raise this issue. However, given the context, it is impossible to believe that don Pedro was robbing his community in any way or that anyone at the time seriously thought he was. Everyone would have known he was paying the shortfall. Of course, it is true that the six-tostón tribute weighed much lighter on his shoulders than on those of the working people, but in their face-to-face community, in which most people knew most other people personally, they probably did not blame him for that. Don Pedro might conceivably have siphoned off some of the profits from the fields planted on behalf of the various churches. But such acts would seem counter to the nature of a man who poured hours into keeping detailed records and who ended up donating substantial amounts of money to various churches when their associated tribute fields did

24. Testament of don Juan de la Cruz, document 5. On the tradition of perorations in the corpus of testaments from the Toluca Valley, see Pizzigoni, *Testaments of Toluca*, 21–22.

25. "Unsigned Nahuatl Materials and a Letter," in Anderson and Schroeder, *Codex Chimalpahin*, 184–239.

not produce enough. Living in the vibrant second half of the seventeenth century, not far from Mexico City, it makes perfect sense to think that he could have made his fortune off the mules we know he possessed, without any need to rob his neighbors, many of whom he was bonded to by ties of blood and affection.

And therein, perhaps, lies the strongest evidence that we are not really seeing deep class tensions—that is, that don Pedro's book indicates that the principales and the tlapaliuque were not separated by an absolutely impermeable barrier. That there were social distinctions seems beyond question. But a man could change his status over the years. In 1658 one Nicolás Gaspar was listed as a witness for the tlapaliuque on the question of whose maguey plants were being sown in the newly plowed field belonging to San Francisco. But in 1669, seven years after his son married don Pedro's daughter, and he himself had attained a certain seniority, he was suddenly elected as an alcalde and later given the title "don." His child Juan could take his wife's surname "De la Cruz" and serve as governor toward the end of his life. In a related vein, it was customary for well-to-do families to take in orphan girls (who were sometimes probably merely poor, not literally orphaned, as the word could mean either) to do domestic work, and the families exhibited a definite sense of responsibility toward these girls, helping them with their marriages and leaving bequests in their wills.[26] There wasn't much that was terribly new in this regard. Traditionally, in preconquest times extensive polygyny among the Nahuas' leading families had created a world in which almost all noblemen were tied to several commoner families, and success in battle or in trade had made it possible for boys from commoner families to rise into the ranks of the nobles.

There is greater evidence of tensions between polities than between rich and poor; when different polities masked older ethnic differences, then tensions could be rife, but when they did not, then even in this regard peace generally reigned. The altepetl of San Pablo Tepemaxalco contained, as we know, eight constituent parts, or tlaxilacalli, and the people within them were mostly interrelated, both literally and figuratively, in such intricate ways that they rarely seem to have defined themselves in opposition to one another. The

---

26. Such young women appear in the De la Cruz papers in 1669 and 1683 and again in the 1691 will of don Juan de la Cruz.

eight political divisions were the organizing rubric of the tribute roll book and seem to have been divided according to geography—that is, if one's main residence fell within a certain physical territory, then one paid tribute in, for instance, Pasiontitlan. But someone, like don Pedro, who paid tribute in Pasiontitlan could find that his residence was very near the church of Santa María de la Asunción and that he often worshipped there. His wife could be from another tlaxilacalli, and so his children could have cousins in several. No wonder the people in don Pedro's book do not appear to harbor hostility to one another based on the tlaxilacalli to which they belonged. Only one time in all his pages did don Pedro lodge a complaint on this basis: in 1665 he said the people of Santa María de la Asunción had got off almost scot-free in preparing for a feast day, paying a small sum rather than contributing labor—and they had nevertheless assumed it was acceptable for them to watch (and enjoy) the bullfights along with everybody else, though others had done much more.

On the other hand, San Pablo Tepemaxalco truly bridled in its relationship with San Pedro Calimaya, the other altepetl with which it made up the greater altepetl that was the town of Calimaya, as the Spaniards called it. Before the coming of the Europeans, we remember, Tepemaxalco was founded by Mexica conquerors to help govern the region. At the time of the conquest, it must have been particularly galling for the once-dominant Tepemaxalca people to find themselves declared by the Spaniards to be a junior partner in the greater altepetl of Calimaya. Those feelings did not entirely disappear, even if people no longer remembered the preconquest origins of the mutual resentments. In 1667 don Pedro complained bitterly that the people of Calimaya paid nothing toward some new furnishings for the main church of the convento of San Pedro y San Pablo, for which the two subaltepetl were supposed to share responsibility. However, the most painful references to Calimaya occur in the 1680s, during the watch of Juan and Josepha. A hated man named Francisco de la Cruz, whom Juan calls an alcalde, must have been from San Pedro Calimaya, for if he had been from Tepemaxalco, he would have been named as a cabildo member somewhere else in the Tepemaxalco record. This man, we remember, had a friend of don Juan's arrested in the 1670s in a move that don Juan clearly understood to be partisan.

It is possible that Francisco was trading on his connections with and knowledge of the Spanish world, for not long before that, in 1672, he was mentioned as being the person who translated for a Spanish census taker. Even all these years later, San Pedro Calimaya was the more populous and therefore senior partner in the pairing, and so the people of San Pablo Tepemaxalco may have been extremely sensitive to the idea—and probably the fact—that the former had greater influence with the Spaniards. Indeed, their fraught relationship may explain don Pedro's and later don Juan's extreme generosity toward the convento's church. Years later, in 1696, a Calimaya man named Francisco de la Cruz, almost certainly the same old enemy, would be ordered by the state to cease and desist in his efforts to interfere with Tepemaxalco's cabildo elections.[27]

Certainly, there was no love lost between the two political units. In 1683, representatives of each went to Mexico City to pick up a quantity of gold that was being donated by the leading hacendado of the area, the Conde de Santiago Calimaya, for a new altarpiece. Neither group could trust the other to bring the treasure home: they split it in half there and then, so each altepetl could bear its own half back to town. Later, after the artwork was completed, they agreed that the people of San Pedro Calimaya would be responsible for cleaning the bottom half of a large new statue, and those of San Pablo Tepemaxalco the upper half. Politics in the old, preconquest world had consisted of endless efforts to keep alliances alive, interrupted by crises that tore them asunder. The potential for rage directed at one's neighbors was always present, most especially, as in the case of Calimaya, when one did not really know those neighbors personally.

---

27. AGN, Indios, vol. 33, exp. 90, 1696, "Se ordena a la justicia de Metepec no permita que el indio Francisco de la Cruz se entrometa en las elecciones de gobernador que pretenden hacer los naturales de los pueblos de San Lucas, Santa María de la Asunción, Santiago y San Francisco Cuajustengo, sujeto a la cabecera de San Pablo Tepemaxalco" [It is ordered that the court of Metepec not permit the Indian Francisco de la Cruz to insert himself in the election for governor that the natives of the towns of San Lucas, Santa María de la Asunción, Santiago, and San Francisco Cuajustengo, subject to the town of San Pablo Tepemaxalco, are trying to hold].

A Place in Spain's Empire

Looming over the lives of the people of Tepemaxalco was the fact that they were required to make not insubstantial annual payments into the coffers of the Spanish state. This reality had become such a basic part of their lives by the middle of the seventeenth century that there is little attention focused on the fact in the text, and were it not for the tribute roll book that Pedro de la Cruz kept alongside his annals-style book, we might imagine that he rarely thought about the matter. We would be making a mistake, however. Even in his annals-style book, he mentions three times in fifty years (1619, 1630, and 1672) that a census taker "came to count people." We are to understand that officials came from Mexico City to check on population counts so that the annual tribute required could be adjusted. The amount that don Pedro was responsible for collecting (1.5 pesos per adult) was substantial for poor farmers who did not have the oxen required to plow large fields and who lived mainly in a noncash economy; we get a sense of what things cost and how much artisans were paid in the pages of the De la Cruz papers, and this was an amount of cash it would not have been easy for them to come up with.[28]

Still, the De la Cruz family papers are not primarily a record of the transfer of wealth from indigenous hands to Spanish ones. Much more than this, they constitute a record of the gradual increase of Spanish influence in the lives of the people of Tepemaxalco. Don Pedro referred to the use of the Spanish court system to settle indigenous quarrels only once in all the years he wrote, but in the late 1670s, after his death, his son-in-law don Juan almost immediately had recourse to Spanish authorities twice in quick succession to settle local disputes. After he was attacked and beaten up, he traveled to Toluca to file a legal complaint, as we have seen, and then, when Francisco de la Cruz from San Pedro Calimaya was "speaking calumnies" against a friend, he waited until the *guardián* of the convento

28. Another way of understanding the impact of tribute for the inhabitants of Tepemaxalco is to consider that the official salary for a day of work in the mines of the area was one-and-a-half reales, and that roughly 50 percent of private contracts for all sorts of jobs in the region did not reach even half a real for the day (García Castro, *Indios, territorio, y poder*, 238–39; his calculations are based on a sample of contracts from the early seventeenth century found in notarial archives).

visited Tepemaxalco the next week and asked him to intervene. In the realm of art and culture, it is clear even in the earliest pages of the manuscript that the Christian church dominated the people's creative outlets, but, at first, the people seemed to play instruments and paint archways in tiny local churches mostly to suit themselves. Yet by the 1680s they were contributing their time, energy, and cash toward an extravagant renovation of the Franciscan convento's church in a project in which Spaniards were directly involved. That was the moment when altepetl representatives traveled to Mexico City, where they met with the area's largest hacendado, the Conde de Santiago Calimaya, who gave them a donation of 300 pesos worth of gold to be used to make the new altarpiece. They bought gypsum and other needed materials, hired Spanish artisans, and eventually even agreed to cook Spanish food for the visiting master painters.

Similarly, in the linguistic arena, we move from a writer who uses few loanwords to writers who use several (verbs like *costarse*, "to cost," which don Pedro had managed very well without), until, finally, in the early nineteenth century, a young Spanish-speaking De la Cruz sets himself the task of translating parts of his grandfather's and great-grandfather's text.[29] He can still do so, with relatively few misunderstandings, but it is clear that his own grandchildren will have lost such ability, since they are obviously no longer hearing the language from even the family's oldest members. The De la Cruz family gave no evidence of feeling oppressed. But it nevertheless remains the case that they were increasingly motivated to rely on Spanish authority figures, to decorate their churches to compete with the chapels of Europe, and to speak the newcomers' language rather than that of their ancestors. Given that they lived within the Spanish Empire, and in a relatively highly trafficked zone, it would be impossible that it should be otherwise.

Yet, although we see increasing Spanish influence, as expected, what is perhaps more interesting is the regional and individualistic flavor, even the uniqueness, of the text itself, fitting no single genre, indicating that people's creativity was not stifled, that they continued to assert themselves in unpredictable and sometimes subtle ways.

29. For more on loanwords in the text, see the appendix, which addresses language and orthography.

And this is very much in keeping with what we know of local indigenous society throughout the Toluca Valley.[30]

Religion

A passionate commitment the De la Cruz family shared across generations was service to the church, in various forms. It all started with music played during mass or for religious festivals and processions. In fact, don Pedro began his public career in the community as an organist, helping with the purchase of an organ and wind instruments for a local church in 1647. Back then he put in 40 pesos of a total 410 pesos that were needed, but this was just the beginning: as governor almost twenty years later, he contributed 400 pesos to buy a new organ worth 500 pesos for Tlatocapan Ahuatitlan, and in 1673, shortly before stepping down, he alone donated an organ to the main church of the convento for the remarkable amount of 650 pesos. All the way through he helped the cantores acquire trumpets, a guitar, and a rebeck, as well as a music score, since he paid for a *villancico* of San Pedro, as mentioned above. His enthusiasm for religious music might have persuaded his father, don Juan de la Cruz, to support the purchase of the organ back in 1647 very generously: he gave 110 pesos toward the 410 total, more than double the amount put down by the governor at that time. Or we may well see in this a genuine interest in music that was transmitted from father to son.

Don Pedro gave more than music to the religious celebrations in Tepemaxalco. As governor, he was ready to supply plenty of expensive candles for processions, especially during Lent and Easter, as well as for the consecration of churches, chapels, and their important art works. In 1664–65 he gave four pounds of regular candles and two pounds of taper candles for the consecration of the side altarpiece of the Virgin in the church of the tlaxilacalli of Santa María de la Asunción, but in fact this was just a small contribution compared to all the rest. He was behind the whole enterprise and paid for the carpenter who executed the work, the material, a bell for the church, the wine, and other essentials for the celebration; he also participated in the purchase of a litter by the local *cofradía* (confraternity). The

---

30. See Pizzigoni, *Life Within.*

items were treasured for years. While the side altarpiece is no longer there, today's church of the Virgen de los Angeles is still a vibrant building in the community, splendidly decorated and displaying a statue of the Virgin now at its central altar. And a litter similar to the one used by the local cofradía can still be seen in the little museum of the main church of Calimaya (see figures 2, 3, and 4).[31] Don Pedro did not fail to take note in his book that, while the people of the tlaxilacalli of Santa María contributed only 21 pesos to the festival, he himself gave a total of 120 pesos. The celebration must have been quite a spectacle, with bells ringing, candles lighting up the church, and even bullfighting for two days. Just four years later don Pedro did something similar, though with even more grandiosity, judging by the money he spent. Another side altarpiece of the Virgin (indeed, another Santa María de la Asunción) was consecrated, this time in the main church of Tepemaxalco, and the image, the carpenters who worked on it, the candles, the gunpowder for the fireworks, and the roan horses were all paid for by him: "It was the gobernador don Pedro de la Cruz who donated it [all]," a total of 300 pesos, more than double the money he presented before. Certainly he had learned a great deal during his early days as mayordomo of the church of San Juan, when he kept the accounts of the expenses of the church and the celebration of the patron saint for the then governor don Diego de la Cruz. Now his accumulated experience and the resources at his disposal magnified his deeds.

Don Pedro also made active interventions in favor of the main church of Calimaya-Tepemaxalco and its convento. The list of his donations is as impressive as the list of his gifts to smaller, local churches, and some of them probably still exist. Today the main church of Calimaya is more modern, but to its left we find the church now called the Tercera Orden de San Francisco (see map 2). It is the oldest one in the whole town and contains a variety of colonial paintings and statues. At the center of its altar, our eyes glimpse a statue of San Francisco, and it may well be the very one that the indigenous parishioners were contemplating in the late seventeenth century,

---

31. We were able to see these elements thanks to the efforts of a deeply knowledgeable resident of Calimaya, Julio César Gómez Hernández.

FIG. 2 Interior of the church of the Virgen de los Angeles in Calimaya, in
what was once the tlaxilacalli of Santa María de la Asunción. Photo: authors.

FIG. 3 Statue of the Virgin in the church of the Virgen de los Angeles. Photo: authors.

FIG. 4 Seventeenth-century litter surviving in the museum of the main church of Calimaya. Photo: authors.

thanks to the contribution of don Pedro de la Cruz to the cult of this saint (see figures 5, 6, and 7).[32]

Don Pedro never slowed down. In 1674, most likely the last year of his governorship, he gave money for the doors of the chapel of San Juan as well as for fixing the church of San Francisco. Furthermore, "the mules of the gobernador don Pedro de la Cruz worked to transport the sand and mud, and he paid those who worked." We have also mentioned how in that same year he petitioned for a chapel dedicated to the Virgin of Guadalupe to be built in Tepemaxalco, offering to cover all the expenses, for a total that remained untold. The permission was granted, conditional on a thorough check on don Pedro's resources. The fact that later in the document we find

32. When we visited in October 2017, the main church of Calimaya was closed in the aftermath of the earthquake that had shaken central Mexico a month earlier. See Loera y Chávez de Esteinou, *Memoria india,* for the Church of the Tercera Orden and more.

FIG. 5 Facade of the church of the Tercera Orden de San Francisco in Calimaya, the original church attached to the Franciscan convento. Photo: authors.

FIG. 6 Interior of the church of the Tercera Orden de San Francisco. Photo: authors.

FIG. 7 Statue of San Francisco in the church of the Tercera Orden de San Francisco. Photo: authors.

references to such a chapel proves that he delivered what he had promised (see map 2 for the site of the modern Capilla de Gualupita, as it is called).[33] Over a time span of roughly twenty years, don Pedro put at least 980 pesos in building, repairing, and adorning the churches of his altepetl and providing the essentials for the festivals of dwellers and visitors alike. Adding this to the 1,090 pesos spent on organs alone, we come to a staggering amount. Whether he was a beloved official we cannot say, but he was certainly an energetic and devoted one.

What we have seen so far tells us of a rather clear choice that don Pedro made in terms of religious offerings: he seems to have been more interested in ambiance or overall emotional experience than in Christian doctrine specifically, as musical instruments and building maintenance and decoration definitely took priority over masses or specific images of saints, for instance. Indeed, saints make only brief appearances in don Pedro's account, often connected to a bigger project, such as the side altarpieces of the Virgin: the money for the image of Santa María de la Asunción was just a part of what he gave for the whole altarpiece and the festival for the consecration. Besides Santa María, Santiago, San Francisco, and Santo Cristo mentioned earlier, during his time as organist and then governor he referred to images of saints on only two other occasions. Once in 1654 he donated a San Juan, and the other time, in 1668, he mentioned a statue of the Virgin, a Jesús Nazareno, and the angel he paid to have painted on the cupola of the same church. Unconnected to don Pedro, we find a reference to an image of San Antonio and a Holy Cross, while more detailed citations of saints occur after his governorship. A close reading of all this material scattered through the De la Cruz document with a focus on saints reveals some aspects worthy of note.

The most prominent images are those of the Virgin and Christ, treated like any other saints, just more popular, and mentioned in different versions: Santa María de la Asunción, Virgen de Guadalupe, Santo Cristo, Jesús Nazareno, and Santo de Jerusalén, as well as the Holy Cross. All this is very much in line with the practice across the Toluca Valley and beyond.[34] As for the other saints, those who

33. See AGN, "Que el alcalde mayor."
34. On Marian devotions and the beginning of the cult of Christ in Spain, see Christian, *Local Religion*, 21–22. On the predominance of the Virgin and Christ among

correspond to the patron saints of the various tlaxilacalli of Tepemaxalco are certainly present: San Francisco, Santiago, San Juan, and
Santa María de la Asunción, besides San Antonio, from a tlaxilacalli
of Calimaya, as well as the patron saints of the double altepetl, San
Pedro (for Calimaya) and San Pablo (for Tepemaxalco). A curious
story hides behind the images of San Pedro and San Pablo, the locally
renowned *pleito de los santos,* or "brawl of the saints." It seems that
when the Spanish unified Calimaya and Tepemaxalco they put on
the main altar in the parish church a wooden statue of San Pedro and
San Pablo, one piece with each saint on one side. From that central
position, only one saint at a time could face the congregation, and
there lay the problem: Who should it be? Each community thought
of themselves as having priority, so when the people of Calimaya
entered the church they would turn the image to have San Pedro
in plain sight, while those of Tepemaxalco would hurry to turn it to
San Pablo any time they could. One day the parish priest, tired of
this competition, took a saw and cut the statue in two, separating the
saints by their back and putting them in two niches. They can still
be found this way today in the church of the Tercera Orden de San
Francisco (see figure 8).[35]

The De la Cruz family was from Pasiontitlan, whose name was
from not a conventional patron saint but the passion of the Christ,
and this may be behind the generous donation that don Pedro made
for a monument for Holy Week. Otherwise, he and his family show
devotion to various patron saints across the tlaxilacalli but not to
the most obvious one for Tepemaxalco: San Pablo. In fact, it was
San Pedro who was at the center of the family's attention, with an
image in the house that was passed down to his son-in-law Juan
de la Cruz. When his turn came, don Juan transmitted the same
devotion and at least one image of San Pedro to his eldest children,
Jacinto and Josepha. In public don Juan showed great support for
both saints of the double altepetl, as testified by all the work and

the Spaniards, see Zárate Toscano, *Nobles antes la muerte,* 168, and Ragon, *Saints et
les images,* 363 (also among mestizos). On the popularity of these cults among indigenous people in central Mexico, see Gruzinski, *Guerre des images,* 285–86.

35. The story is reported in Loera y Chávez de Esteinou, *Memoria india,* 41–47.
She mentions that the story has been passed down orally for centuries, and the details
(i.e., the name of the parish priest or when the separation happened) are not known.
Our local guide in 2017, Julio César Gómez, also referred to the story.

FIG. 8 Statues of San Pedro and San Pablo in the church of the Tercera Orden de San Francisco. Photo: authors.

resources he put into the *retablo* (altarpiece) of San Pedro and San Pablo in 1683. But in the privacy of his testament, among the numerous sacred images that populated his house and were passed on to his children, the town's patron saint of San Pablo is nowhere to be found. Thus, don Juan offers a remarkable example of why the idea of the cult of patron saints needs to be reconsidered. While the patron saint certainly had an important role in community celebrations and identity, it seems that behind the door of the household, personal choices and preferences, as well as the names of family members, played a key role in deciding which sacred images were venerated. The Spaniards could divide a town and declare who was to worship which patron saint, but they could not ensure that the people would truly devote themselves to that saint more than to others of their choosing.[36]

One aspect concerning the saints is the connection they had with land, an intriguing trait of indigenous society across central Mexico that is not seen in the Spanish counterpart. A couple of references in the De la Cruz text point to a fascinating possibility, while the analysis is backed by a wealth of examples in indigenous testaments.[37] San Juan, a favorite saint for don Pedro de la Cruz as well as for Tepemaxalco more generally, is said to have a little tribute field at Pelaxtitlan, from which money came in 1660 to buy two corncribs to store the saint's harvests. Over twenty years later don Francisco Nicolás, past alcalde of Tlatocapan, left a plot of land to the Virgin of Guadalupe, to be planted with her magueys.[38] In practice a community or an individual would donate a piece of land to a saint, with the expectation that either the group or a family member would cultivate it, with the harvest sold and the profits put into the worship of that saint or another religious deed. This way a saint became a de facto owner of land and, in many cases, inherited a parcel like any other family member or individual connected to the testator. The purported words of don Pedro invoked by a relative more than a century later, in 1795, speak directly to this: "I, don Pedro de la Cruz, gobernador of Tepemaxalco [have passed? or lent?] to señor Pascual López this land to break and sow for a few years, and when he leaves it, the lord Santo Santiago the Apostle will get it, and from tomorrow onward nobody is to take it away from him."

The details regarding the saints in the De la Cruz papers allow us a glimpse into the materiality of sacred images in people's lives. They were usually painted, either on a church wall, like Santiago

36. This argument was first made in Pizzigoni, *Life Within*, 170–71 (see also Wood, "Adopted Saints," 278–79), and more recently in Pizzigoni, "Church and at Home," in Nord, Guenther, and Weiss, *Formations of Belief*, 106–25. Saints different from the patrons were also present, in smaller numbers, such as San Bernardino and Santa Clara, as well as numerous angels. In the examples we have from the Toluca Valley, angels are treated like saints in representation through sacred images and worship. See Pizzigoni, "Where Did All the Angels Go?," in Cervantes and Radden, *Angels, Demons, and the New World*, 126–45.

37. See Lockhart, *Nahuas After the Conquest*; Wood, "Adopted Saints"; and Pizzigoni, *Life Within*.

38. Other references that may give away possession of land on the part of a saint include San Francisco's 1679 tribute corn that gave money to buy the church canopy.

the Apostle or the angel on the cupola, or else on a lienzo or canvas, like San Francisco at the central altar of the main church. That they could also be statues is revealed by the fact that individuals donated clothing and ornaments for them, as in the case of Santa María de la Asunción and Jesús Nazareno, both in the main church. Here details are lacking, but normally the statues were of stone or wood. Any of these images would have cost thirty pesos minimum, judging by the fragmentary information in the document—quite a significant sum, if we consider that the common value of smaller images that individuals kept in their home was three to six pesos, while sums around twenty pesos were deemed unusual.[39]

Finally, there are two references to a retablo, typically a complex vertical structure behind an altar that mixed both painting and sculpture. In fact, the two side altarpieces of the Virgin mentioned earlier could well be considered a sort of retablo, with statues or sculptures. And the church of the Tercera Orden de San Francisco that still stands to the left of the main church of Calimaya preserves a fine example of one to this day (see figure 9). Thanks to the rather meticulous account of governor don Juan de la Cruz, we know that behind the retablo of the holy sacrament and San Pedro and San Pablo, again in the main church of Tepemaxalco, there were at least two painters, one gilder, and over a month of work. Among the essentials required there were three pounds of *bol de castilla* (a compound used for gilding), four pounds of gypsum to make plaster, 3 pesos worth of glue, dyes for 7 pesos, and papier-mâché for the flesh of the angels, as well as food for two craftsmen. Apparently, don Diego Castillo, master painter, and Miguel de Blancas (probably less skilled, since he had no title) were of Spanish descent, considering the title *señor* as well as some of the food they ate: saffron, Castilian oil, olives, vinegar, garlic, cinnamon, and shrimp. They were both given 120 pesos, while another craftsman, known only as Tomás, was given 7 pesos for gilding and no food, perhaps because he was a local or completed his task in a short period. These are valuable, rare details, for, generally, information about church artisans is often lost in the historical record.

39. On canvases, statues, and prices, see Pizzigoni, "Church and at Home," in Nord, Guenther, and Weiss, *Formations of Belief*, 106–25. Notice the different language used for Santiago and San Francisco in the De la Cruz document, on which the assumption that the former is painted on the wall is based.

Their work must also have involved some maintenance of the main altar, given that toward the end of the entry for the year the cleaning of a statue of Santo Cristo, and of San Bernardino and Santa Clara on the tabernacle (*sagrario*), is mentioned. All together, the community put a great deal of money into this enterprise, and it came from the 150 pounds of gold that don Juan de la Cruz, together with three officials, collected from Conde de Santiago in Mexico City. But the governor invested his own money as well, at least 80 pesos and three weeks' worth of food for the master painter. And an investment it certainly was, given that through it don Juan perpetuated the De la Cruz family as committed and devoted rulers of their altepetl.[40]

A walk down the alley of the main church of Calimaya-Tepemaxalco in one of the celebrations allowed the people to contemplate these beautiful works of art, shining even in the darkness by the light of ever-present candles or silver lamps. Such images would accompany their devotees for generations, as the examples of San Antonio and Santa María de la Asunción illustrate. Set up in the main church in 1654 and 1669, respectively, they were still there in 1691–93 and 1710, when don Juan, his son Jacinto de la Cruz, and later Jacinto's wife, Polonia María, asked to be buried in front of them. Many of these images, and the churches that guard them, have been preserved to today. They are more than preserved, as a matter of fact: they are still at the center of lively celebrations and heartfelt worship, as the statues of San Pedro and San Pablo show, especially during their feast on June 29.

Nor was it just the visual element that lasted. Even the accompanying world of sound remained somewhat familiar as time went by. As long as the De la Cruz family members kept their record, the making and recasting of bells for the chapel of the Virgin of Guadalupe took up much ink, almost certainly an activity that increased in importance over time, given that to this day there is an active workshop for bell making in Tepemaxalco.[41] And then there was the music, still very much at the center of the De la Cruz family a century and a half after don Pedro and beyond. On August 7, 1809, the last

---

40. The other reference to a retablo is a very short one, for the blessing of the retablo of San Antonio, and in this case it may imply just a small painting, not the full structure.

41. Personal communication from our guide, Julio César Gómez Hernández, October 2017.

FIG. 9 Retablo in the church of the Tercera Orden de San Francisco. Photo: authors.

complete entry of the document, don Bernardino Cruz y Serrano paid for the repairs to the organ of the church of Guadalupe.[42] Whether he could actually play it, as don Pedro once did, is not clear; however, don Bernardino showed the same zeal as his predecessors toward religious music and perhaps even a bit of self-righteous irritation concerning the family's perennial communal duties. He noticed that it was not the first time that the organ needed repairing, and the person who did it "charged for his work forty-five pesos, on top of all the materials that I gave him, so for all it was sixty pesos." It would seem that in Tepemaxalco's spiritual life, as in its sociopolitical arrangements, the more things change, the more they stay the same.

42. Clearly, the chapel started by don Pedro de la Cruz with his 1674 petition became a landmark of the Tepemaxalco community, and its people were still providing resources for its fixing and additions in 1809. AGN, "Que el alcalde mayor." Moreover, a cofradía based at the chapel is mentioned in the litigation papers among which the testament of don Juan de la Cruz was found; in the year 1772 it is said that the chapel was founded by don Pedro de la Cruz and that the Virgin could count on land that was hers for over forty years. AGN, Tierras, vol. 2533, exp. 5, 1772–73, "Autos seguidos a pedimento de Felipa de la Cruz, vecina de Calimaya, contra Antonio de la Cruz, mayordomo de la cofradía de Nuestra Señora de Guadalupe en el pueblo de Tepemajalco, fundada por Pedro de la Cruz" [Proceedings following the request of Felipa de la Cruz, resident of Calimaya, against Antonio de la Cruz, mayordomo of the confraternity of Nuestra Señora de Guadalupe in the pueblo of Tepemaxalco, founded by Pedro de la Cruz].

[fol. 1]

1647[1]

v Axca inpan i meztli a 6 de Jullio de 1647 año yn itechconpa teontlatquitl ynhua tlapitzalli ynhua organo nica momachiotia ca tehuan nican tictzinpehualtia maestro **mathias de S. fransico ynhua p°e de la crus + organista nican tictohuechihuilisque in ixipatzinco in Dios ynhua in no cequiti omotlahuechiuhque**[2]

v Jua de la crus + yn oquihuechihua yntechcopa organo maCuilpohuali ynpa matlaCtli

_____ 110 p°s

v ynhua p°e de la cruz + organista oquimohuechihuili onpohuali p°s

_____ 40 p°s

v mathias de S. fran°° maestro matlaCtli p°s oquihuechihua

_____ 10 p°s

v don baltensal de los reyes gōr onquitemaca opohual p°s ypa matlaCtli p°s yntechcopa organo

_____ 50 p°s

v ynhua tlapalique matlaCtli p°s oquihuechiuhque

_____ 10 p°s

v gabriel de S. p°e sepohuali p°s oquihuenchihua ytechcopa organo

---

1. Certain years are inserted in another, probably later, handwriting. They are represented in italics.

2. Certain sections are presented in larger, darker lettering, as if intended to be understood as the beginning of a section. They are represented in bold.

_____ 20 pᵒs

v Juana Salome viuda Sepohuali pᵒs oquihuechihua ytechcopa organo

_____ 20 pᵒs

v Angelina franᶜᵃ matlaCtli pᵒs oquihuechihua

_____10 pᵒs

v baltensal de S.tiago maCuili pᵒs oquihuechihua

_____5 pᵒs

v pᵒe Juachi maCuili pᵒs oquimohuechihuili

_____5 pᵒs

v yhua catores yepohuali ynpa matlaCtli³ pᵒs ontemacaque ytequimil ytech oquis

_____ 70 pᵒs

[fol. 1v]

v yhua Sa lucas tlacatl matlaCtli pᵒs oquimohuechihuilique yntechcopa organo

_____10 pᵒs

v yhua oc ceppa omoconpahui sepohuali pᵒs ypa matlaCtli pᵒs yc oniquixtlahuili se quixtiano

_____30 pᵒs

v mochi omocetlali ynpan ica setzotli ynpan matlaCtli pᵒs

_____410 pᵒs

Titofirmatia tehuantin

	Don baltensal re [sic] los reyes, gōr
Don Juan de la cruz +	pᵒe de la cruz + organista
mathias franᶜᵒ maestro	grabiel de s. pᵒe
Juana Salome	Agelina [sic] fraᶜᵃ
baltensal de s.tiago	pᵒe Juachi

v timochti tictlalia tofirma amo quemania quitosque Aço mochi tlacatl oquicouhque organo, ca ça quezqui tlacatl onquicouhque

[fol. 2]

1652

_v_ Axca inpa xihuitl 1652 año yntechcopa totequimil topelaxtitla ça tehuan onticyelimique

notatzin Jua de la cruz + ~~allde~~ ynhua nehuatl pᵒe de la cruz + organista yua grabiel de s.pᵒe yua franᶜᵒ de la cruz + sa

_____

3. *MatlaCtli* may actually read *maltlaltli*, and, if so, it represents a regional pronunciation we have not seen before.

ontlapalehui—quezqui tonatiuh yua yn quemania amo acan quitos:
Aço altepetl oquicouhque canmara ca sa tehuati otitochicauhque
timacuili tlacatl yua sa ome xihuitl ontitopalehuique yua sa oc
tomexti ontitochicauhque notatzin Jua de lan [sic] cruz + yua nehuatl
p°e de la cruz + organista ynpa xihuitl: 1654 año yn otipixcaque
tlaolli omonamacac ca onicalaqui yca on[mo]copahui Sancto San
Juatzin caxtoli p°s: yhua yc omocohua tlapali caxtoli p°s yc omicuilo
teonpa, omocetlali cepohuali p°s yua matlaCtli p°s

_____30 p°s

v yhua yca oniquipalehui mitotian yca oticcouhque garçonis
[calzones] matlaCtli p°s yuan ome p°s yua yca omoxtlahuia yc
omitzomo ce p°s yhua nahui tomi

_____ 13 p°s 4 tomi

destigos don adres de s.ta maria   p°e hernades Juez mayor
Jua martin topile ~~allde~~   nicolas p°e escribanos
1656
v Axca ynpa xihuitl 1656 años yntechcopa yc omochiuh cuezcomatl
amo quemania quitosque Aço altepetl oquichiuhque ca sa
tehuati catores otitochicauhque oticchiuhque cuezcomatl tehuati
oticpopoloque ome p°s yuan ome tomi yca tiquixtlahuilique
quauhxiqui Jua de la cruz + S.n atonio —Jua de sa migl calimaya

_____ 2 p°s 2 ts

v yua nehuatl p°e de la cruz + onicponpolo Se p°s huel
onicmocuitlahui cuezcomatl yua grabiel de s.p°e amo quemania
quitosque aço yehuati oquichiuhque tlapalique ca ça otlapalehuique
yc omitzoma cuezcomatl ça quezqui tlacatl oquauhhuilaque axca
Sancto S. Juatzin ytlaol ca çan omocalotiz [will be stored] axca
niquicuilo amatl ypa xihuitl 1657 año   i p°s
[fol. 2v]
franᶜᵒ hernadez alhuasil mayor catonres= matheo Nicolas topile yua
yehuatin catores Nicolas Juseph diego bernardon p°e Juachi y grabiel
de s.franᶜᵒ diego xacobo ymixpan
1655
v Axca inpa xihuitl 1655 año ynpa meztli a 18 de octubre
intechcopa in comotlapo:⁴ tlalli san franᶜᵒ amo quemania

---

    4. It seems we are seeing the presentation of a glottal stop at the start of the
word *comotlapo*. The writer is inconsistent in this regard.

quitosque aço mochi tlacatl [osancamoque?] ca ça quezqui tlacatl:
ontequipanoque nica nestiyez
   teonpaquiyahuac
<u>v</u> grabiel de tapia sen yota
<u>v</u> Juan baptt^a ce yota
<u>v</u> Jesu Nicolas ce yota
<u>v</u> fran^{co} Nicolas ome yota
   paxiotitla
<u>v</u> Don p^oe de la cruz + mayordomo de sancta yglesia maCuili yonta
<u>v</u> Don Jua de la cruz + biudo ce yota
<u>v</u> p^oe de sanctiago ce yota
<u>v</u> diego de la cruz ome yota
<u>v</u> diego xacobo ce yota
   tlatocapa
<u>v</u> Jua Pablo ce yotan
<u>v</u> Jua matheon ce yotan
<u>v</u> Jua Moreno ce yotan
<u>v</u> fra^{co} de la cruz + chicome yotan
<u>v</u> betora de S. Jua ce yotan
   puchtla
<u>v</u> Jua martin alhuasil mayor ome yota
<u>v</u> Jua baptt^a ce yota
<u>v</u> mathias de s.fran^{co} ome yota
<u>v</u> Luyz damia ce yota
<u>v</u> mathias fran^{co} alhuasil mayor ce yota
omocetlali sepohuali yua matlactli yota yua yey yotan

_____33 yota

[fol. 3]
<u>v</u> ynhua tlapaliuhque Acan amo quimopielia yotan: sa
cemilhuitequitl sa yehuatl oquihuicaque huitzontli sa quezqui
tlacatl otequipanoque: Amo quemani quitosque: aço mochi tlacatl
otequipanoque ca yehuatzin Don p^oe de la cruz + mayordo^[mo] Sancta
yglesia omochicahuacn [sic] yntequipa Do diego de la cruz + gōr yua
do graviel de s.p^oe ~~allde~~ Sevastia xacobo rexidor mayor Jua de la cruz
+ esnos axca ocalac ypa libro yntequipa don p^oe de la cruz +
1657
<u>v</u> **Axca miercoles a 10 de octubre de 1657 años nica machiotia**
yc mosancamo tlalli sa fransico ytenquipa yehuatzin Don p^oe

de la cruz + don grabiel de sa p°e ~~allde~~ sevastia xacobo rexidor
mayor melchio xpoval rexidor nicolas de sa p°e esnos
   teompaquiyahuac

<u>v</u> Don grabiel de s.p°e ~~allde~~	Jua baptta ce yota
<u>v</u> fran^{co} nicolas ce yota	fra^{co} xayme ce yota
	Jua matheo ce yota

1658

<u>v</u> **Axcan ynpan i xihuitl 1658 año: omosacamo tlalli sa
francico: oc tepetzin ytequipa don p°e de la cruz gōr** cen
yotan −Jua Moreno se yota−Jua matheo ce yota−Lucas margos ce
yota−yhua tlapaliuhque Aca amo quimopielia yota ca ça yehuatl
oquihuicaque huitzouhtli amo quemania quitosque aço mochi tlacatl
oyelimique ytequipa yehuatzin don p°e de la cruz + gōr don grabiel
de s.p°e ~~allde~~−Jua fran^{co} rexidor mayor Juan baptt^a rexidor−luys
damia Jues−nehuatl onitlacuilo nicolas de s.p°e esnos−nehuatl
nictlalia−no firma namotlatequipanocatzin
[fol. 3v]

1658

<u>v</u> **Axca miercoles a 10 de octubre de 1658 años
motlatlanilisque anço yehuati oquiçacamoque tequimilli nica
sa frasicon ca nehuatl noyota yūa** nocayaniz oyellimique yhua
oquitlalique metl yaxca quezqui tlapaliuhque yhua nehuatl ca noaxca
nauhpatli nehuatl onictlali metl Don p°e de la cruz + gōr
Amo quemania quitosque aço mochi yaxca altepetl oniquitlatlanili
amo yaxca oconaque Jurametin calaquizque destigos Adres de
s.miguel Jues−diego xacobos−Jua baptt^{as}

Juan Rafael	nicolas gaspal	grabiel de s.fran^{co}
fra^{co} hernadez	melchio xpoual	don diego de la cruz + pas.do gōr
fran^{co} Nicolas	d grabiel de s.p°e ~~allde~~	nehuatl onitlacuilo
		nicolas de s.p°e esnos

mochti destigon tlapaliuhque yua cinhuame ymixpa omicuilo yn
amatl cihuatepixque Juana hernadez
<u>v</u> Axca ynpa xihuitl 1658 años omohuecapano cuezcomatl=
oquitilaque quauhhuitl catores amo tlapalique oquitilaque
quahuitl amo quemania tle quitosque yaxca a 16 dias de octobre
otlapalehuique diego xacobo= adres nicolas−Juan martin−bernaber
totonri−Sevastia quauhxique oniquimaca ome tomi ytequipa
yehuatzin nehuatl onitlacuilo nicolas p°e esnos

1658

v Axca ynpan i xihuitl 1658 años a 14 de enero: omitzoma cavuarion yntequipa yehuatzin don pᵒe de la cruz + gōr

v Axca savado a 19 de enero omitzoma Sancto Sa franᶜᵒ yn ichatzinco yhua tenextli omocouh maCuili hanega yntequipa yehuatzin Don pᵒe de la cruz + gōr

v omoquez tequicalli Sa franᶜᵒ oquiquezque tlapalique Sa Pablo tepemexalcon

v ynhua Sa lucas tlacatl otlapalehuique

v ynhua Sancta maria Asupcio tlacatl otlapalehuique ytequipa yehuatzin Don pᵒe de la cruz + gōr

[fol. 4]

v Año

1607	**Axcan ynpan i xihuitl 1607 años omomiquili gōr ocatcaya Don buenabetora de clemete**
1608	
1609	
1610	nican omoquetzinno gōr Don franᶜᵒ min
16ii	franᶜᵒ felipen esnos
1612	
1613	
1614	
1615	
1616	nica omoquetzinno gōr don daniel balquez ycha san atonion
1617	
1618	nica oponpoca⁵: huey citlalli a 10 de octubre yhua oqualoc [i]n tonatiuh
1619	nican otenpohuaco Juez de la cueta xpoual de medranos
1620	mayordomo [a]lasanro garsian
1621	
1622	
1623	
1624	nican omoquetzinno gōr Don Jua bapttᵃ ~~allde~~ don baltesal Re [*sic*] los reyes
1625	nican omoquetzinno gōr don baltensal de los reyes oqualoc [i]n tonatiuh otlapoyahuan

---

5. What we call a *comet* they understood as a star leaving a trail of burning smoke. The form appears in a variety of poetic ways in the annals.

1626
1627
1628
[fol. 4v]
1629   Axca a 26 de mayo oncehuetzin huel oponpoliuh y toctli
1630   nica ontepohuaCo Juez de la Cueta yntoca: almiraten
1631   nica omoquetzinno gōr don mathias fran^{co}
1632
1633
1634
1635   Axca a 24 de fefrero chicahuac omochihua cepayahuitl yn
        ipa ylhuitzin san mathias apostol[6]
1636   a 2i de junio omocahuati quauhpatli Atego onca Sa fra^{co}
        oti[c]quixtique[7]
1637
1638
1639   huel chicahuac otlalolini
1640
1641
1642   onpeuh concoliztli huel chicahuac
1643   a 4 de Agosto ypa ylhuitzin Sancto domigo huel oponpoliuh
        toctli quiyepehua tlaxilotin
1644
1645
1646   Axca savado a 6 de enero oquiz totlaçonatzin
1647   Axca a 6 de marzo nica oticpehualtique teonpa Sancta
        maria: omomiquil gualdia fray baltensal
1648
1649
1650   nica omochiu Sa fran^{co}
165i   A 24 de febrero huel ce cemana oquiyahui
[fol. 5]
1652
1653   Axca ynpa xihuitl 1653 años yn itechcopa yc omicuilo Arta
        mayor titohuechihuilizque yxpatzinco y dios nehuatl p°e

---

6. In Aragón the saint's day of Saint Matthias the Apostle is indeed the twenty-fourth of February.

7. We have some doubts about the intended meaning here.

de la Cruz + yhua Jua de la Cruz + yhua fran^{co} de s.tiago
amo quemania aca quitos: aço altepetl oquichiuhque ca ça
tehuatin otitlahuechiuhque yhua otiquiCuiloque Sanctiago
yhua corro tepitzin yhua llienço S. fran^{co} –nehuatl p^{o}e de la
Cruz + yepohuali p^{o}s ynhua matlaCtli p^{o}s onicnohuechihuili

_____ 70 p^{o}s

_v_ yhua yn cani moquezticac Sancto Christo çano nehuatl
onicchiuh: yhua cielo oponpoliuh chicuey p^{o}s

_____8 p^{o}s

_v_ yhua Jua de la Cruz + oquihuechiuh cepohuali p^{o}s yua
yeye p^{o}s

_____ 23 p^{o}s

yhua fran^{co} de Sanctiago oquihuechiuh caxtoli p^{o}s

_____ i5 p^{o}s

_v_ yhua teonpatlacatl oquiCuiloque organo oquitlalique:
oonme [_sic_] tomi otlapalehuique yhua mathias de s.fra^{co}
oquihuechiuh ome p^{o}s yhua nahui tomi

_____ 2 p^{o}s 4ts^o

yhua yntoca diego bernardo oquihuechiuh maCuili p^{o}s

_____5 p^{o}s

omocetlali chiquacepohuali yua yey p^{o}s nahui tomi

_____ 123 p^{o}s 4t

_v_ Achtopa oquimotlalili ynfirma padre guardia yhua
tehuatin tictlalia yn tofirma

mathias de S.fran^{co} maestro	p^{o}e de la Cruz + organista
Jua de la Cruz +	fra^{co} de s.tiago—yhua topileque
Fran^{co} hernadez	Jua de s. m̄īḡl

1654   Axca domigo a 4 de enero omoteonchihua Retablo S.n
atonion

1655   nica omoquetzinno gōr don diego de la cruz + Axca domigo
a 6 de Junio—1655 años onipehualtin niquiCuiloa= yhua
ynic onictlamic niquiCuilohua yn arco yn teonpa calitic oca
ocalac tomi oponpoliuh chicuey p^{o}s nehuatl p^{o}e de la Cruz +

_____8 p^{o}s

[fol. 5v]

1655   nima don Jua de la Cruz + notatzin oquihuechiuh ome p^{o}s

_____2 p^{o}s

<u>y</u> nima Sa Juatzin yc omoquez y teocaltzin yhua yc otzoquiz
yc nitlapalehui matlaCtli p⁰ˢ nehuatl p⁰e de la Cruz +

_____10 p⁰s

auh yn Sa Jua ymiltzin oniquixti caxtoli p⁰s

_____ 15 p⁰s

Çano yehuatl ytequimiltzin ytech oquiz caxtoli p⁰s

_____ 15 p⁰s

yhua yc onicopahuic nima yc omicuilo yca mochi cepohuali
omatlali [sic] p⁰s nehuatl p⁰e de la Cruz +

_____30 p⁰s

nima yc omicuiloc ça nehuatl oni[c]quixti yno tomi ynic
omicuilo teonpa calitic caxtoli p⁰s

_____ 15 p⁰s

don baltesal de los reyes yhua yno franᶜᵒ de la Cruz + yn
oquihuechiuhque yca mochi maCuili p⁰s yuan ome tomi

_____ 5 p⁰s2 t⁰s

nima lucas margos catol [cantor] oquihuechiuh tlapali yc
omocouh yc omicuilo lienço

_____5 p⁰s

ynixpa tlatoque nehuatl oniquifirmati p⁰e de la cruz +

Don diego de la cruz	don grabiel de s.p⁰e	Sevastia xacobo
+ gor	~~allde~~	regidor mayor
melchio xpoval	mathias de s. franᶜᵒ	p⁰e Juachi alhuasil
rexidor	maestro	mayor
		Jua de la cruz + esnos

niman yc nohuiya xolarpa macehualtzintzinti yn
oquihuechiuhque aca oome tomi aca nanahui tomi anoço
aca oquihuechiuh= ce p⁰s—yca mochiuh yn oponpoliuh
napohuali ocaxtoli p⁰s yuan ome tomi

_____ 95 p⁰s2 t⁰s

<u>y</u> oc omocouh tomi oc cepohuali yua maCuili p⁰s yca
omochiuh yn ilhuitzin S. Juatzin amo quemania quitosque
Aço mochi onicponpolo yn itomitzin Sa Juatzin nehuatl
notoca p⁰e de la cruz+ onicnocuitlahui yn ichantzinco Sa
Juantzin nimochiuhtica nimayordomo Sancta clesia yua
matlaCtli p⁰s yuan ome p⁰s yca omochiuh miSSa fiesta
yeyti totatzintin oquichiuhque miSSa yua yn inacayotzin
otiquixtlauhque ome p⁰s yua nahui tomi ypa xihuitl 1655

años ytequipa don diego de la cruz + gōr axca lunes a 24 de Julio=

oniquichihuili Cueta	don pᵒe xacobo	fraᶜᵒ hernadez
diego xacobo	fraᶜᵒ martin fiscatl	Adres de s. mīḡl
luyz damian	adres nicolas	Jua baptista

amo quemania motecueposque

1656   nica omoquez gōr Don mathias de s.franᶜᵒ
[fol. 6]

1657   nica omoquetzinno yehuatzin gōr Don pᵒe de la cruz +

1658   ycc ome xihuitl çano yehuatzin omoquetzino gōr don pᵒe de la cruz + Axca domigo a 19 de mayo omohuilana quauhpatli Atego axca Juebes a 2i de febrero oylpiloque doyā maria de medosa

1659   oc ceppa omoquetzinno gōr don pᵒe de la cruz + Axca viernes a 3 de enero ypa nahui ora otlalolini huell iquac otiacique omopatla tlatohuani[8] don pᵒe de la cruz + gōr = axca Savado a 4 de enero occepa otlalolin ypa ce ora Axca [i]n ipan xihuitl 1659 años catonres ytomi nicpieya yca oncopahuique sacabochi yhua sen quitaran yua cen raber[9] mochi oponpoliuh tomi Aoctle y: niquipielia ynpa xihuitl 1657 años omopixcatlaoli yc omommacac ce hane[ga] chicome tomi

_v_ Axca domigo a 9 de febrero 1659 años omocouh ce bribiario ypa tlaoli oquis maCuili pᵒs yua ce pᵒs yc oquipaleaqualdia[10] ynpa xihuitl 1658 años yntequipa grabiel de s.tiago maestro yhua yehuatzin don pᵒe de la cruz + gōr

—————————————————————————— 6 pᵒs

don franᶜᵒ min ~~allde~~ nehuatl onitlacuilo Jua pblo esnos
_v_ yhua ynquac omocopahui Sancto Christo onpa oniquixti ce pᵒs yc omocouh
asente ——————————————————————————

    1 pᵒs

<hr />

8. Although we have translated as we have for the sake of clarity, this phrase literally states, "when we came to changing our _tlatoani._"

9. _Raber_ is for _rabel_ (rebeck).

10. We are not certain what to make of this unusual formation, but we think we have been true to the general sense.

yhua pitol yca onicohuili ycac sano oca oquiz matlaC tomi
yntoca bernador—omocetlali mochi oponpoliuh chicome p°s
yhuan ome tomi nehuatl onitlaCuilo Jua pablo esnos

_____7 p°s 2 t°s

yhua catores aço capa oquiquixtique   yey p°s yua nahui
huetzintli yc oquicopahuique sancto xp̄o
tomi oquihuenchiuhque

_____ 3p°s 4 t°s

v Axca ynpa xihuitl 1659 años quin omocouh yey almaro[11]
ypatiuh matlaCtli p°s yua yey p°s yua chicome tomi

_____ 13p°s 7 t°s

Yhua sonbrano chiquace quin omocon ynpatiuh nahui p°s
yua ome tomi

_____ 4 p°s 7t°s

yua ca onpa oquiz tomi capa titentlaneltia bestido: onpa
oquiz tomi
Axca Savado a 28 de Julio oniquimacac tomi catores chicome
p°s yc oquicouhque tropeta mayor maestro fra^co hernadez
yua diego xacobo alhualsi mayor nehuatl notequipa Don p°e
de la cruz + gōr

_____7 p°s

1660   occepa omoquetzinno Don p°e de la cruz + gōr
Axca Juebes a 22 de abril 1660 años otiquixtlaque yey
p°s yua nahui tomi ypanpa cadela ypa quaresma omonec
ynpa pro [fol. 6v] sancion sacnto christo—catores nehuatl
onitlacuilo—Jua Pablo maestro matheo nicolas topile

_____3 p°s 4 t°s

v Axca Juebes a 24 de junio i660 años yn tehuati
teonpatlacatl cuicanime ca tictemaca matlaCtli p°s
ytech pohui Sancta crusis + ytotlaçotemaquixticatzin y
topanpa ytech omomiquiliztzinno y titlatlacohuanime ma
tictomahuiztilica Amo quemania acan quitos ca notomi ca
y tequimetl catores onpa oquinquixtique yua tlapaliuhque
cano [sic] nahui y metl oca oncalac Amo quemania acan
quitemos ca nica tictlalia tofirma

_____10 p°s

Don p°e de la crus +

---

11. *Almaro* is probably for *armario*, a wooden wardrobe or cupboard.

fra^co hernades maestro pas.do

matheo nicolas topile
y nehuatl nitlacuilo Jua
Pablo maestro

nehuatl nixpa
feliphe de la cruz + esnos[12]
yhua oc mocahua caxtoli p°s _____ 15 p°s
yhua ome p°s otechmomaquili Sr. do p°e de la cruz + gōr
yc oticonque miSsa yhua y bilacico san pedro ytech oquis
tlaolli tenhuati oticonaque tomi fran^co hernades matheo
nicolas topile nehuatl Jua Blo [sic] maestro

_____ 2 p°s

Sn Lucas

Axca miercoles a 19 de mayo i660 años yquac omomacac
porcecio tlalli sa Lucaz yehuatzin don p°e de la cruz + gōr
oquimotemaquili matlaCtli p°s onticmacaque Sōr ~~allde~~
mayo don astasio

_____10 p°s

yhua sano yehuatl gōr oquimotemaquili se p°s yua nahui
tomi Jua de aquilol nahuatlatoc oquimomaquili

_____i p°s 4t°s

yhua tlatlasqui chiquace oquimotemaquili gōr ce p°s yua
nahui tomi ypatiuh

_____i p°s 4t°s

Yhua poyos ce docena otemaca yc otitetlapalohua metepec
yua mexico

_____i p°s 4t°s

yhua yey tomi otemaca yc oquitlalique cuetlaxtli madamieto
yua cetica xuchitl

_____ 4 t°s

yhua oquimotemaquili gōr yey tomi yc omocuh [sic]
queson; ometica yua binagre yua asete nahuitica mochi:
chiucnahui tomi

_____ 9 t°s

occepa oquimotemaquili gōr matlaC [sic] tomi

_____ 10 t°s

---

12. The names are so crushed together that we cannot be certain of the order
intended or even who was past officer and who was present.

yhua se ycapoti gōr yquac otiaque Atego otipaltique ypa
Viernes teontla onca callitic ayac omocuitlahui: asta [fol. 7]
ynpa Lunes yn yoma gōr oquiquixti quiyahuac oquiçohuato
onca: onquiqualique pitzome ynpanpa ynquac omonemilli
tlalli: San lucas yxtlahuacan axca omosetlali oquiponpolo
yehuatzin Don p°e de la cruz + gōr caxtolli p°s yua ce p°s
yhua ce tomi yhua ce yncapotin

_____16 p°s it°s

don Pablo de s.tiago	don xpoval de	frac^{co} martinez Juez
allde	s.graviel allde	
nehuatl onictlacuilo	feliphe de la cruz +	nehuatl nictlali
	esnos	nofirma atonio
		Jusephe
		esnos

<u>y</u> Axca domigo a 1 de Agosto i660 años oticconque yey
camara: yn patiuh matlaCtli p°s yhuan ome p°s yua ome
tomi ynpan oquiz ytomitzin Sa Juatzin tepitzin tequimili
mopie pelaxtitla yhua se camara yehuatzin oquimocohuili
So⁻r Don p°e de la cruz + gōr yaxca Amo quemani quitosque
aço mochi yey yaxca

_____ 12 p°s 2t°s

1661   yc macuilli xihuitl occepa omoquetzinno gōr don p°e de la
cruz + inquac omochihua pleto=
Axca ypa xihuitl i66i años omopixca ytlaoll catores
chiuhnahui hanega yc omonamaca se garja nahui p°s

_____ 9 hanega

1662   yn¹³ chiquace xihuitl occepa omoquetzinno: gōr do p°e de
la cruz + chiquace meztli otequipano: yhua don Jua Pablo
omochiuh no chiquace meztli
Axca miercoles S.ncto a 5 de abril i662 años omochiuh
procecio: onticonque cadela chiquace libra yhua se p°s
oticmacaque totatzin onquichiuh prosecio mochi omocetlali
chiquace p°s yhuan ome tomi

_____6 p°s 2 t°s

yhua yc omocopahui tropeta nahui p°s nitemaca

_____4 p°s

---

13. This and the next year's entry really seems to read *yn* instead of *yc*. If it is not
an error, then the writer switched from using ordinal numbers to cardinal numbers.

yhua ome p°s onitemacac yca oquiconque Amatl ypa metl
oquiz

_____ 2 p°s

yhua onitemacac caxtolli p°s yca omocouh bazo[14] ynpa metl
oquiz tomi

_____ i5 p°s

Axca ypa xihuitl i662 años omopixca ytlaoll catores caxtolli
hanega

_____ i5 fanega

[fol. 8]

1663   in chicome xihuitl omoquetzinno gōr don p°e de la cruz
        + omocehui pleton ypan imihuitzin sanctosme Juebes
        chicahuac oncehuetzin huel occe qualo Sitli
        Axca miercoles sancto a 2i de março i663 años omochihua
        proceciom omocouh cadela chiquace libra yhuan ce
        p°s omomacac totatzin yn oquichiuh procesio: mochi
        omocetlalli chiquace p°s yhuan ome tomi

_____ 6 p°s 2 t°s

        Axca ynpa xihuitl 1663 años omopixca catores yn itlaor
        [space left for amount but never filled in]

1664   in cchicuey [sic] xihuitl omoquetzinno gōr don p°e de la cruz +
        v Axca lunes a i5 de setiebre i664 años nica momachiotia
        yntechcopa quauhxiqui yntonca baltesal paxqual mayeço
        oquimoximilli: totlaçonatzin SAncta ma.ª Apsucio yn
        icolatelaltzin ytlaxtlahui sepohuali p°s ynhua maCuilli p°s
        yaxca gōr tomi

_____ 25 p°s

        yhua oc yey p°s oquimotemaquili çano yehuatzin yaxca gōr

_____ 3 p°s

        v yhua omotemaquili caxtolli p°s yc omoxtlahua colatelal
        yehuatzin tomi gōr do p°e de la cruz +

_____ i5 p°s

        yhua yquac omoteonchihua colatenlar onquiponpolo:
        caxtolli p°s yuan ome p°s yehuatzin don p°e de la cruz + gōr

_____ i7 p°s

---

14. *Vaso* appears as the musical term "base" in Covarrubias Orozco, *Tesoro de la
lengua castellana.*

yhua cadela nahui libra yhua ome libra mogia[15] mochi
ynpatiuh nahui p°s yua se tomi sano yehuatzin yaxca tomi
gōr don p°e de la cruz +

_____ 4 p°s i t°s

yhua tlapalli yhua tisal yua tzac[u]tli ynhua ytlaxtlahuil
pitol mochi matlaCtli p°s sano yehuatzin yaxcatzin tomi gōr
don p°e de la cruz +

_____ 10 p°s

yhua omotemaquili yey garga tenextli ypatiuh yey p°s sano
yehautzin yaxcatzin tomi don p°e de la cruz +

_____ 3 p°s

yhua yquac omocohua Andan[16] omotemaquili maCuilli p°s
yaxcatzin tomi gōr

_____ 5 p°s

yhua cen capana omotemaquili sepohuali p°s ynpa caxtoli
p°s ynpatic S.no yehuatzin yaxcatzin tomi don p°e de la cruz
+ gōr

_____ 35 p°s

yhua se arova bino omocohua ynpatiuh chiquace p°s sano
yeyehuatzin [sic] don p°e de la + gōr oquimotemaquili

_____ 6 p°s

[fol. 8v]
La Asumpcion

omocetlalli yn oquimotemaquili yehuatzin gov Don
p°e de la cruz + chiquacepohuali p°s ompa santa maᵃ
Asupcion Amo quemania motecuepazque yhua amo
quemania quimahuispolosque ynpilhuatzintzin noço
yxhuihua axca ypa xihuitl i666 años yc matlaCtli xihuitl
yc motequipanilhuiya gor Don p°e de la cruz + nehuatl
onitlacuilo atonio Jusephe esnos

_____ 120 p°s

1665   occepa omoquitzinno don p°e de la cruz+
Axca domigo a ii de octobre i665 años omoteonchiuh yn
iteocaltzin yhua yn icolatelartzin totlaçomahuisnatzin
ome tonatiuh omahuiltique tondo otitechieque tenhuati
onficiales

15. *Mogia* is used for *bogia* or *bugia*, a tapered candle.
16. *Andan* is used for *andas*, a frame or litter for carrying an image.

Don pºe de la cruz + gōr

Do mathias franᶜᵒ alde Jua baptta alde   Do pºe hernadez alde
Jua mn Juez mayor   migl serano fiscatl

         Atonio Juseophe esnos

yhua sancta maᵃ tlacatl amo tley oquitlalique tomi san
ixquich yc oquichiuhque fiesta cepohuali pºs yhua se pºs yc
otechieque

_____ 21 pºs

yhua yn comonamacaque¹⁷ bagas ynpatiuh yehpohuali
pºs yehuatl oquimocahuiliti don baltensal de los reyes gōr
ocatca

_____ 60 pesos

ynhua se adan omocohua ynpatic sepohuali pºs yua caxtoli
pºs confrarias yn itomitzin totlaçomahuisnatzin mayordomo
migl serano nehuatl onitlacuilo Atonio Jusephe esnos

_____ 35 pºs

[fol. 9]

i666   Axca inpan i xihuitl i666 año ocsepa omoquetzinno Don pºe
de la crus + gōr
_v_ Axca savado a 7 de março i666 años oniquicohuili
sacabochi catores ynpatiuh caxtolli pºs ynpa metl oquis
omichiqui yehuatl maestro loreço lopes fraᶜᵒ xayme alhuasil
mayor yehuatzin yntequipa Don pºe de la crus + gōr nehuatl
onitlacuilo atonio Jusephe esnos

_____ 15 pºs

yhua yehuatzin Sor Don pºe de la crus + gōr yaxcatzin tomi
oquimohuechihuili nahui pºs yua ome tomi

_____4 pºs 2 tºs

_v_ Axca Juebes a ii de febrero i666 años ticchihuilique
cueta: catores yn itomi chicuepohualli pºs yua matlaCtli
mochi tlacatl ymixpa amo quemania motecuepasque nica
ticmachiotia ytenquipa Seᵒʳ don pºe de la crus + gōr nehuatl
onitlacuilo feliphe de la crus + esnos

_____ i70 pºs

yhua opohualli pºs yc omocon sacabochi yua Bazo yua Amatl

_____ 40 pºs

---

17. Again, a regionally typical glottal stop at the start of the word _comonama-caque_ is rendered visible to us.

Axca ynpan i xihuitl i666 años oticcalaquique
maCuilpohualli p°s yc omocohua organo y tehuati catores
ynpa metl oquis tomi

_____ oo 100 p°s

Tenhuati titofirmatia tixpa ynquac omochihua cuetan
Don fra^{co} min fiscatl
<u>v</u> y yehuatzin mahuistililoni S^r don p°e de la crus + gōr
oquimonextilili yn iaxcatzin yn dios quimoxtlahuilia yn
ipanpa organo quimotemaquilia macuilpohuali p°s tixpa
tehuati ticatores nehuatl notoca loreço lopes maestro
ninofirmatia
diego bermado alhuasi mayor—Gaspal melchio ahuasir
mayo pas.do—frac^{co} xayme alhuasir mayo pas.do—diego
xacobo alhuasir mayor—diego serano topile—grabiel de S.
fran^{co} topile—nehuatl onitlacuilo Antonio Jusephe esnos—
don Matias fra^{co} alde—don Jua min alde—feliphe de la crus
+ esnos

[fol. 9v]

<u>v</u> Axca ynpan i xihuitl i666 años nica sa Pablo tlatocapa
ahuatitla nica momachiotia yn itechcopa organo ca
yehuatzin Sor Don p°e de la crus + gōr oquimohuechihuili
cetzontli p°s yhua catores macuilpohualli p°s oquitemacaque
omocetlalli mochi ypatiuh cetzotli ynpa macuilpohualli p°s
nica neztiyez ynpa ylhuitzin sa Jusephe omoteonchihua
ynpa de março a i9

_____ 500 p°s

Do mathias de s. fra^{co}		Don Jua martin, alde
alde		
Don atonio Juarez,	Don grabiel de s.	fran^{co} hernades rexidor
alde	p°e, alde	mayor
Fra^{co} mathias	luyz damia	
alhuasir mayo	mayordomo	

nehuatl onitlacuilo feliphe de la crus+ esnos[18]

1667   Axca ynpan i xihuitl 1667 año occepa omoquetzinno gōr
Don p°e de la crus +
<u>v</u> Axca ynpan i xihuitl i667 años omoteochihua poerta yua
algo huey teonpa cobento ynpa ylhuitzin S.tisimo sacrameto

18. Some of these must have been past *alcaldes*, though it is not indicated.

a 9 de Junio amo comonidad yncapa oquis tomi ca yehuatzin
Sor Don pºe de la crus + gōr oquimohuechihuilitzinno
yxpatzinco yn dios nauhpohualli pºs yca mochi tetzotzoque
ynhua quauhxique amo quemani quitosque altepehuaque
aço comonidad oquis tomi

_____ 00 80 pºs

yhua calimaya tlacatl atley oquitemacaq⁻ tomi san ixquich
otetlaqualtique yhua yehuatzin gōr oquitlaqualti ometi
mayeço ytoca Roque flores yua ce ytoca Jua blas mayeço gōr
oquiponpolo matlaCtli pºs yhuan ome pºs yca tlaquali

_____ 12 pºs

ytequipa Don pºe de la crus + gōr—do mathias de s. fraᶜᵒ
alde Don Pablo de s.tiago alde grabiel de tapia rexidor mayo
Juan aloso rexidor Adres nicolas Jues nehuatl onitlacuilo
felipe de la crus + esnos omocetlali nepohuali pºs yua
matlaClti yuan ome pºs nica nesties

_____ 90 pºs 2 pºs

[fol. 10]

v ynhua poerta sachristia no yehuatl otictlalique yacuitl
ycxin tepostli omotlalli ypatic ome pºs yua alraua[19]
ypatiuh yey pºs yua nahui tomi sano yehuatzin Sᵒʳ gōr
oquimohuechihuili

_____ 5 pºs 4 tºs

1668 Axcan inpan i xihuitl i668 año ocsepa omonquetzinno
yehuatzin gōr Don pºe de la cruz +
nica momachiotis yehuatzin Sōr Don pºe de la cruz +
gōr oquimohuechihuilitzinno teonpa yn itlaquetzin
totlaçomahuisnatzin—yhua bovenra[20]—yhua tenextli
cohualoni yhua Agel ynpa bonbera yn omoquez ynhua
maSanis yhua quauhxique yn itlaxtlahuill mochi omosetlalli
oquiponpolo chiuhnapohuali pºs yhua chicome pºs yua
nahui tomi nica neztiyez

_____ 187 pºs 4 [t]

v ynhua yehuatzin Jesus naSareno opohuali pºs yhua
matlaCtli pºs ypatictzin

---

19. *Alraua* is used for *aldaba,* generally a knocker but can be a metal door handle
with a latch.

20. *Bovenra* is used for *boveda,* a vault or cupola.

_____[blank]

_v_ yhua yornametotzin

_____[blank]

_v_ yhua sen lapra ynpatiuh chiquacepohuali p°s yaxcatzin
Jesus naSareno *Tiene once marcos y tres onzas de Plata. El
Plato con que se colectan los Jornales y Limonas sera tres
marcos y quatro onzas de Plata. Y es de Jesus Nazareno.*

_____120 p°s

_v_ yhua yn ibacotzin²¹ totlaçonatzin Asupcio yntlaxtlahuill
quauhxiqui yhua pitol omocetlali mochi yepohuali p°s

_____ 60 p°s

[fol. 11]

1669   Axca inpan i xihuitl i669 Años ocepa omoquetzinno gōr
Don p°e de la cruz + don fra^co marti ~~allde~~
Axca nica momachiotia ytechcopa totlaçomahuisnatzin
Asupcio: omoteonchihua yn icolatelartzin ocalac huey
teompa mochi Echora²² yhua quauhxique yn itlaxtlahuill
yhua ynquac omoteonchihua cadela cohualoni yua borbora
yua Rohuera²³ mochi omoSetlali oponpolli caxtolpohuali
p°s ypa febrero a 24 ypa yn ilhuitzin= sa mathias Apostol
omoteochihua ca yehuatzin gōr Don p°e de la cruz +
oquimohuechihuilli

_____ 300 p°s

Alcales [*sic*] ymixpa

Do fra^co min ~~allde~~   do nicolas gaspal   don atonio Juarez
                    ~~allde~~   ~~allde~~
                    nehuatl onitlacuilo feliphe de la cruz + esnos

_v_ Axca Jueves a 2i de marzo i669 años nica momachiotiz
yn itoca Jusepato: otichuapanque nica yntic calli
omohuapahua=axca omonamictique ytonca diego de s.tiago

1670   Axcan inpan i xihuitl i670 Años ocsepa omoquetzinno
yehuatzin Don p°e de la cruz + gōr Jua min ~~allde~~

---

21. *Ibacotzin* is probably used for *banco,* a seat or stand.
22. *Echora* is used for *hechura,* an image.
23. *Rohuera* is probably used for *polvora* (the powder needed for fireworks) and
ruana (roan horses, needed for the procession in the streets).

167i Axca inpan i xihuitl 167i año omoquetzinno Don mathias de
sa frasisco + gōr ~~allde~~ Do Pablo de sa Jua Do grabiel de tapia
~~allde~~

[fol. 11v]

Año

1672 Axca inpan i xihuitl 1672 año ocsepa omoquetzinno gōr Don
p°e de la cruz + ~~allde~~ Don Jua min Don fra^co hernades ~~allde~~
do migl serrano ~~allde~~ feliphe de la cruz + [rubric] ynpan i
xihuitl 1672 año ontepohuaco Juez de la cueta= Do diego
de guidos de huadalajara ~~allde~~ mayor yehuatli mochihua
Juez yhua secretario Don p°e [illegible] de noba nahuatlatol
Fran^co de la crus
mochi otechcalaquili ynpa padron : açusion tlacatl

1673 Axca inpan i xihuitl 1673 año occepa omoquetzinnno gōr
Don p°e de la cruz + ~~allde~~ Don Jua min= Axca ipan i xihuitl
1673 año yhua se monometo ynpa semana sancta omonequi
yehuatzin Do p°e de la cruz gōr oquimohuechihuilitzinno
ypatiuh opohuali p°s yua caxtoli p°s

—————————————————————————— 55 p°s

_v_ Axca savado a 22 de Julio 1673 años se organo
omquimohuechilitzinno yehuatzin Don p°e de la cruz
+ gōr onpa huey teonpa cobeton ypatic se tzotli ynpa
matlaCpohuali yua onpohuali yua matlaCtli p°s

—————————————————————————— 650 p°s

ynhua puerta canpila sano yehuatzin
onquimohuechihuilitzinno gōr ypatic onpohuali p°s ypa
xihuitl de 1674 año

—————————————————————————— 40 p°s

_v_ yhua louan²⁴ ome p°s ynpatic

—————————————————————————— 2 p°s

[fol. 12]

1674 Axca inpan i xihuitl 1674 año ocsepa omoquetzinno gōr Don
p°e de la cruz + ~~allde~~ Don Jua min Don migl serano ~~allde~~
Don Jua diego ~~allde~~ axca inpa meztli a 24 de agosto 1674
años omotlali puerta ychatzinco sancto Sa Juatzin ynpatic
onpohuali yua matlaCtli p°s mexico onpa omochihua Sa

24. _Louan_ is used for _ruana_ (carriage horses or roan horses for processions).

Juatzin ytomitzin yca omochiua moxti ymixpa oficiales ca
yehuatzin Don p°e de la cruz + gōr oquimocuitlahui

_____50 p°s

v yhua chapa

v yhua Sancto Sa fran^co yn iteonpachatzinco Axca ynpan i
xihuitl de i674 año omochichihua⁻ teonpa yehuatzin Sōr
Don p°e de la cruz + gōr oquimohuechihuili opohuali p°s

_____ 40 p°s

yhua ymolahua otequipanoque = oquisansacaque xali yua
tlalli yua y cayanixti ontequipanoque san oquimotlaxilique[25]
ayac omochicahua San icel oquimocuitlahui gōr Don p°e de
la cruz +

~~axca domigo a i5~~[26]

v axca domigo a i5 de setiebre y de i678 [sic] año nica
momachiotia Santa ma^a asusion tlacatl oquipouaco
matlacpouali ypā naupouali peso yxpātzinco Don Ju° min
gov

don niColas blas alde   D. migel serano alde

don adres garsia alde pas.do   D.n atonio Juares fiscal pasdo

fra^co diego Regidor mayor

nehuatl onitlaCuiloa Lore[n]so de satiago esnos

nehuatl oni[c]seli tomi D. Ju^a de la cruz alde matlacpuali ypā
naupouali p°s

28°p°s

[fol. i2v]

v Axca Domigo a i5 de çetienbre i678 años nican momachiotia Santa
maria açusio tlaca: oquicahua ompohualli peso nehuatl
nicçellia tomi Don Ju° de lla [sic] Cruz Allde ymixpantzinco
mochtintzintztin tlatoq'

<u>Son 40 pes^a</u>

Don Ju° min gōr Don nicolaz blaz   Don migel serano Alde
Allde

Donn adres garsia Alde pasado   Donn atoyo [sic] Ju°res fiscal pasado

                                          Fran^co Diego rexidor menor [sic]

Lorenso de Santiago hes^no

---

25. James Lockhart believed the word *oquimotlaxilique* was an error, the intent
being *oquimotlaxtlahuilique*, and we can see no other way to interpret it.

26. A very different handwriting begins here, after a four-year break.

[fol. 13]

v Nyca momachiotia: yn ipa xihuitl: 1677 años yua ynpa metztli De
Junio: a 2 DiaS: ypa ylhuitzin S. Juaᵒ viernes ohuetzin [fell]
ytlaçoylhuitzin: onechpehualti nitelolo huel onechmictiquia
nehuatl: Dõ Juaᵒ De la Cruz + ~~allde~~ De orDinario:
nica nestiyes: yua Sano huell iquac omopehualtico:
nomonatzin omoyetzticatca Doñana: Juᵃ: Sano huel ipa
ytlaçoylhui S. Juᵒ Bauptista: amo oquichiuh çe çemana:
omomiquilli: miercoles: Jueves otictotoquique nehuatl: yua
nocihuahuatzin Dõn Juçepa de la Cruz +: nica nestiyes
v yua nica nicmaxiotia: onia Toluca: ninopati huel occepa
onitlanahuito: huel onihuecauh opa Toluca ca yc
onicmaxitito ye omomiquillique: ometi notexhua matheo
Juarez yua felipe de la cruz + yua ce narmana: cathalina:
auh çatepa omomiquili notlaçonatzin omoyetzticataca:
maria Salome ca mochi ypa yno xihuitl: omochiuh yn nican
momachiotia nica huel nestiyes
v çano yquac ypa xihuitl 1677 años: oquimahuispoloque nocopadre
Loreso Lopes maᵒ²⁷ paçado oquimahuizpolo: francᵒ de la cruz
+: ~~allde~~: oquitzaCuili otlica: tlayohua: ypa chicome ora yua
aqui oquimahuispolo nocopadre:omolpi teylpiloya mestepec
nica nestiyes
v no nica nestiyes: yn iquac oquiquiçtilisqui coro catores yn iquac
otlahuiquiz y nica: ypa toaltepeuh: S. peᵒ y S. Pablo: yehuatl:
tetlatolmacaya francᵒ ~~allde~~ y tlacamoelua²⁸
[fol. 13v] oninochicauh: onicnotlatlauhtili guardia fray Juᵃ
Bauptista: asta: ynpa ocçe çemana omochiuh fiesta; ypa
y çemana nica catores tepemaxalco ça mochi ypa xihuitl
omochiuh nica miCuilo yhua [sic] -- 1677 años

1679 Nyca momachiotia yn iquac: omocouh pallio ynpa xihuitl
1679 años ypa otlato oquimonemilli omomacac chicua çe
pohualli peso ihuan matlactli peço ic opa oquis yn tomi yc
omo[co]uh: S. francᵒ ynpa yntequitlaoltzin: omonamacac
yepohuali peso: ynpa tequimetl: omocobraro çepohuali pˢᵒ

27. *Maᵒ* is used for *maestro de capilla,* as revealed in the entry for 1679.
28. This illegible word is probably *tlacamaneloa* (to mumble). The preceding
verb, *tetlatolmaca* (to give bad advice, to speak calunnies) is rare but found in Molina,
Vocabulario en lengua Castellana, 109v.

Doña Clara Leonor: oquichic: tequimetl: yua nicolas fran^{co}
yua nehuatl Do Jua° De la Cruz + ~~allde~~ paçado oninohueti:
opohuali peço yua matlatli peso yn iquac otiqualicaque
ynpa metztli: De setiebre a i5 dias omoestrenado[29] yquac
otlathuiquis nica nestiyes ayac aqui quemania quitos tley
v yua nica niquitlalia: aquique ynixpa yn iquac ohualo palio:
Destigos timochihuasque mostla huiptla: ytla ytla tley
quitosque: yehuati tlatosque yntech mochi cahuilis: y Dios:
ytlaçonatzin çihuapili Sta ma^a

v Don pe° De S.tiago ~~allde~~ paçado	*v* Don abroçio De S. Ju° ~~allde~~ paçado
v Don loreço Lopez ma° De capila	*v* Diego felipe mayor ^{mo}
v melchor fra^{co} *v* marCus De S.tiago	*v* lucas De S.Ju°

[15v?]

Memoria yn itechconpa miCantzintli sevastia JaConbo huehuetzin
ynn iquac omomoquili ytley yN opopolihui Nican
momachiotitias ynpa xihuitl De 1668 años Anbito
ynpantiuh matlactli peso yua n ome p°s ypatiuh12 p°s

v Nima tlaoli omonec se hanega ynpantiuh se peso   i p°s 4 t°s
    nhua nahui tomi

v Nima CaDela conhualoni se libra chiconme tomi   7 t°s
    ynhua se boregon otictemacaque ypatiuh chiquase   6 t°s
    tomi

    omocetlalli mochi yn opoponliuh Caxtolli p°s yua se   15 p°s 1 t°s
    tomi

Nehuatl onquimillo jusenpa fra^{ca} onechcanhuilitia se tlali opa
matica quauhteco nima se San Lucaz octli opa mantica
sacantzotetitla amo quemani Aqui tlein quitos ca yteconpa
noColltzin CatCan Sanbastia Xacobo can hipan yn itenquipa
y notlasontatzin Do pedro de lan Cruz + gor Don grabiell
De sa pedro ~~allde~~

San luCas ~~allde~~
Do Pablo de S.Jua

Nehuatl nitlaCuillo Don niConlas De sa pedro es.banos

[fol. 16]

v Axca Juebez a 19 de marçon ypann i xihuitl De 1682 añoz ypa
    yey ora huel chicahuac otlallolli huell oquichiuh media ora
    yc oquis huell ipan ilhuitzin s.^{nto} s.ⁿ Josep ytiepo S^{or} don

---

29. *Omoestrenado* is the classic use of a Spanish verb.

Simo Allde ma° guardia fray Ju° bhtt^a ÇeCretario do pe°
Rodriguez nican sā Pablo tepemexalco momachiotia yni
libro ytequipātzinco Don Ju° de lla Cruz + g^or D° lloreso
llopes Ald or°

Don nicollas blas Alde S^a llucas   Donn atonio Ju°res Alde asopsi°
Don Sebastia serano Alde Santiago   fra^co nicollas Rexidor manor
Donn aDres de S.^n ^tiago hesño p° ^co

[fol. 16v]

_v_ Axcan miercoles a 3i de março ypan xihuitl de 1683 Años
nican san Pablo tepemaxalco tlathocapan nica tictlallia
hescritura nehuatl notoca Don fran^co nicolas Alde pasado
noçihuauh teresa fran.^ca yxpantzinco dios niquitohua: Ca
notlanequillistica: yca mochi noyollo nicnomaquillitiaz
çe xollal y notlaçomahuisnatzin nuestra S^ñora huadalope
yhua yn itlaçomahuisconetzin Jesus naçareno: onca
quimotoquillilisque yn imetzin: amo aqui tle quitos
yn quemania: ca noyoloncacopa nictemacatiuh – Axca
nomiquilistenpa yhua nicnohuechililia matlactli metl: ypan
ticalaqui santo cofradia. nehuatl. yhua nosihuauh yhua çe
ycnotlacatzintli ytoca Jusepan: ymixpantzinco
mochtintzintzin tlatoque: nictlalia nofirma yhua notoca
don fran^co nicolas. Alde pasado. teresa fran^ca tehuati
tialtepepixcatzintinhua y tt° dios

Don Ju° de lla Cruz + gor   Don lorenço lopes Alde or°
Don Diego gonsales fiscal mañor   Senora Ayala gonsales hespanolla
destigo

Nehuatl nitlacuilohua ytecopa cocoxqui donn adres de
S.tiago hesp.^no

[fol. 17]

_v_ Axcan miercoles a 3 dias del mez de ffebrerro ypann i
xihuitl de i683 añoz—Nican san pablo tepemaxalco
Ahuatitla—tlathocapan—Nican ticmachiotia yni llibro yn
itechcopatzinco y Retablotzin yn santisimo sacramenton
yhua yehuatzintin santon san pe° san pablon ynic
micuillotzinnozque nica nextiez yn tlen popoliuhtiaz
amo quenmania tlen quitozque y maçehualtin tehuantin
ticmachiotia yni llibro tialtepepixcatzintzinhuan yn tt°
dioz –don Ju° de lla Crus + g^orr Don lloreso llopiz —Alde
Donn agustin diego —Alde dom nicollaz blas —Alde don

migel çerrano —Alde don sebaztia çerrano —Alde don diego
gonsalez. fizcal —don tomaz de lla cruz + Rexidor manor —
Antoyo de loz santoz Rexidor —Nicolaz fran^{co} mañordomo
—Nehuatl nitlaCuillohua donn adrez de s.thiago es^{no}

_v_ yn iquac otiaque mexico oticCuito teoCuitlatl otechmomaquillito
yehuatzin S^{or} conde de santhiago caxtolpohualli llibroz
tehocuitlatl otictoxelhuique calimaya tlaca oconaque
chicopohualli yhuan matlactli llibro sanno yuhqui nican
tepemaxalco oticonaque chicopohualli yhuan matlactli
llibroz.

_v_ yhua oticCohuato yey llibras bol de caztilla^{30} ypatiuh nahui pes^{o}
yhuan nahui tomi ypan comonidad oquiz nican nezties
_____ 4 ps^{o} 4 t
_v_ yhuan tzauhtli oticouhque yey pes^{o}tican
_____ 3 pe^{so}

[fol. 17v]

_v_ yhua chimaltisatl oticouhque nahui llibra ypatiuh se pe^{so} yhuan
nahui tomi
_____i ps^{o} 4t^{o}s

_v_ yhuan tehuanti oti[a]que mexico don Ju^{o} de lla Cruz + g^{or} Don
lloreço llopiz a̶l̶l̶d̶e̶ Don Nicollaz blaz Alde Don çebaztia
çerrano Alde opopollihuato mexico yey pe^{so} yhuan nahui
tomi oquiquato tlatoque
_____ 3 ps^{o} 4t^{o}s

_v_ Axcan sabado a i3 de ffebrero i683 años opeuh
motequitillitzinnohua S^{orr} Don diego Castillo maheço pintor
ca san nehuatl oninohuenti yey çemana onicnotlaqualtilli
nehuatl don Ju^{o} de lla Cruz + g^{orr} Donnã Juçepa fran^{ca}
gobernadora amo quenmania aquin tlen quitoz yn
maçehualtzintzintin

_v_ Axcan martes a 2 de março omohuicac mexicon don nicolas
blas Alde san lucas omotlacocohuilito yn tlen intetzinco
monequis maheçoz pintorres nica nesties
_v_ Omocohuato media harroba hasucar ypatiuh yey ps^{o} yhuann ome

30. *Bol* is the Spanish name for a clay compound used by gilders.

tomi_____3 psº 2 tsº
v yhuan cacahuatl nahui llibran
ypatiuh _____2 psº 4 tsº
v nahuitica canellan

_____
_____ 4 tsº
v yhuan rroballo michi ypatiuh
_____ 2 psº 4tsº
v media harroban camaron ypatiuh
_____2 psº 4 tsº
v yhua ome pesº yhuan nahui tomi llantexas
_____ 2 psº 4 ts
[fol. 18]
v yhuan çe pesºtica frijoles
_____ i pesº
v yhuan chiquaçentica asafran
_____ 6 tsº
v ometica pimeintan
_____ 2 tsº
v ome quartillo açete de castilla ypatiuh
_____ i psº
v ometica haçetunas
_____ 2 tsº
v ometica vinagren
_____ 2 tsº
v cetica ajoz
_____ I tsº
v Axcan biernes a i8 de marçon i683 años nican ticçentlallia ynin
    Cuentan ynic otictotlaxtlahuillique Sᵒʳʳ Don don [sic] diego
    castillo maheçon otictomaquillique chiquaçen pohualli psºz
    nica nesties amo omochiuh derama³¹ ca mochi comonidad
    ypan oquis amo aquin tlen quitos yn quemanian
_____ Son ioo2o psº
v yhuan yehuatzintin Sᵒʳ migel de blancas ontiquitomaquillique
    sanno yxquich chiquaçen pohualli pesºz
_____ ioo2o psº

31. *Derama* is used for *derrama*, a shared tribute or tax.

_v_ yhuan yehuatzin S^{orr} Don Ju° de lla Cruz + g^{orrr}
oquimohuenchihuillique napohuali pes°z oquimocahuillique
Donnã Juçepa fran^{ca} goberndadorra

_____ 80 ps°

_v_ yhuan huel yehuatzin san^{to} s.pablo ynic oquimotlaquetilitzinnoque
tlapacohualoni yc cecni consierto omochiuh yca chicome ps°

_____7 ps°

[fol. 18v]

_v_ yhuan yehuatzin santo x͞p o huel nepantla moyesticati
huellacpac sano tiquixcahuique nica tepemaxalco ynic
omochipauhtzinno yca chicuey ps°

_____8 ps°

_v_ yhuan san bernadino yhuan santa clara yn ipa moyetzticate
sagradio yc omochipauhtzinnoque ometintzintzin chiquaçen
ps°

_____6 ps°

_v_ yhuan tomas ofisial yc otlateocuitlahui oticmacaque chicome ps°

_____7 ps°

_v_ yhuan fran^{co} de lla Cruz + oticmacaque macuili pes°

_____5 ps°

_v_ yhuan nacayotl ynic omonacayotitzinnoque agelles ypatiuh ome
ps° yhuan chiquasen tomi nica nesties ypan comonidad
oquis

_____2 ps° 6 ts°

[fol. 19]
Pesaron las Lamparas de la Parroquia: Jesus y San Juan Sincuenta y
ocho Marcos, las que se dieron por Donativo en 2 de octubre
de 1810.

Maya

[fol. 21]
Ypan xihuit de # 1733 = Yhua = xihuit de 1734 años omochiutzino
Gobernador= D: Nicolas de la Cruz

_____

Yhua pan xihuit de 1743 años omochiutzino G^{or} D: Nicolas de la Cruz =
Axca ypan yni sihuit = de 1745 años ocsecpa omochiutzino
G^{or} Dⁿ Nicolas de la Cruz = Yhua Nica nesties Ypan Yni gasto
timotenquixtia omochiutzino Se santo Jerosalen Yanquicatzintli
ocostaroc ypatictzin senpuali peso Yhuan Nica nesties

oquimotemaquili yc omotlapalehuilique: Santo san lucas
ypilhuantzitzin se peso omotlapalehuilique _____ 1 pˢ
[fol. 21v]
Santa Maria la asumpcion omotlapalehuilique se peso
ypilhuantzitzin alcaldes _____ 1pˢ
Santo Santiago apostol quaxoxtenco omotlapalehuilique
ypilhuantzitzin alcaldes Yca se peso _____ 1 pˢ
Santo San franᶜᵒ puxtla Ypilhuantzitzin omotlapalehuilique Yca se
peso nica nesties_____ 1 pˢ
yhuan Nican toaltepetzin Santo San pablo tepemaxalco tlatocapa
Ahuatitlan Cabesera otictlalique matlactli yhuan chiquasen
pesos _____ 16 pˢ
yhuan noyhuan nican nesties momachiotia ytehcacopa ycamisatzin
Santo Jerosalen
timotenquixtia ohualac Sⁿᵗᵒ San Phelipe y Sⁿtiago tlamimilolpa
oquimoxtlahuilique ypilhuatzitzin ytehcopa quactlalli nahui pesos yc
omocuylitzinoc ycamisatzin _____ 4 pˢ
[fol. 23v]
[Spanish translation of facing page, signed by Manuel de la Cruz +
Serrano, 1842]
[top line missing] . . . la capanas de la capilla de la santicima Virgen de
Guadalupe que fueron fundidas por segunda ves. Los Fabrico
mi Segundo Abuelo D. Nicolas de la Cruz + y Serrano.
Oy Dia Miercoles ha 9 de Marzo de 1746 años cuando haManecio
se acabo de Fundir las dos capanitas de nuestra Señora de
Guadalupe. E en este vario de san Pablo tepemaxalco llo el
Mallordomo D. Nicolas de la Cruz Gobernador Actual Y
haqui enpiesa los Gastos y haqui estan pareciendo:
Conpre una Roba y tres libra de metal consto sinco pesos
. pˢ . . .5. . . . . .tˢ
y tanbien otra arroba
. . . . . .3. 1
y tanbien 3 libras, estaño importo dos pesos un real y medio
. . . . . .2. . .1. . .⊥
y le dí de comer al campanero dos pesos y medio real
. . . . . .2. . . . . .⊥
y cuando Fue la Bendición tres pesos y dos rreales
. . . . . .3. . . . . .2. . .

y tanbien Ferié otra canpanita mediana le dí de [ribete?] veinte y dos pesos

...............22..........

y pagué las dos canpanas qᵉ las yçe nuevas le dí el Maestro D. Migel albares

  treinta y sinco pesos

....35...................

y lo que monta en la cuenta de todo los Gastos y hase la cantidade setenta y dos pesos y seis reales

....72...........6

y tanbien digo llo D. Nicolas de la Cruz y mis sobrinos Francisco de la Cruz y antonio de la Cruz y lo ysimos y lo trabajamos ese dineros con qᵉ pagamos las [can]panas D. Abraccio de la Cruz dió de limosna tres rreales y D. clemente cuatro rreales y la copié oy Dia Jueves a Dies de Nobienbre de 1842.

[fol. 24]

AxCa mierColes Ypan chicnahui tonati[u] de marzo xihuitl de 1746 años Yquac otlanes otlami mofundirua canpanas ome y Nra Sᵃ de de [sic] guadalupe Nican ypan yaltepetzin santo sⁿ Pablo tepemaxᶜᵒ Nehual nimayordomo Dⁿ Nicolas de la Cruz Gᵒʳ Auctual yhuan pehua nogasto Nican nesties: oNiccuh Se aRoba metal ypatic yhuan yey libras maquili pesos ocostaroc _____5 pˢ

yhuan ocse aRoba ypatic yey peoso yhuan se tomi _____ 3 pˢ i toˢ

yhuan maquili libra estaño ocostaroc ome pesos yhuan se [i]hua melio_____ 2 pˢ i to i m

yhuan yc onitlamcac canpanero ome pesos yhua melio_____ 2 pˢ i mᵒ

yhuan yc omochihua bendisión yey pesos yhuan ome tomí _3 pˢ 2 toˢ

yhuan yc onicpatla ocse canpana achi teptzin onitzontic sempoali yhuan ome pesos 20 2 pˢ

_____

yhuan yc oniquixtlahua yn ome Canpanas onicchihua yanquic onicmaca maeso ytoca miguel de albares = senpoali yhuan caxtoli pesos _____ 30 5 pˢ

[fol. 24v]

Yhua quimontarua de mochin no gastos quichihua yepoali yhua matlactli yhuan ome pesos yhuan ciquasen tomi=

  Son 70 2 pˢ 6 Rˢ Dⁿ Nicolas de la +[sic]Gʳ

Yhuan tiquitoa nehual Dⁿ Nicolas de la Cruz Governador

yhua nosobrinos franᶜᵒ de la Cruz yhuan Antonio de la Cruz

oticsenchihuaque otictequipanoque ynon tomi yc omoxtlahua
canpana=

D^n Ambrosio de la Cruz omohuentique yey tomi _____ 3 R^s

D^n lucas Cleme^{te} = omohuenti nahui tomi _____ 4 R^s

[following is in same hand and accompanying same rubric as
Spanish text above]

*En el año de 1829 ha 25 de marzo se bajo la capanita de la capilla de la
Sma Madre de Guadalupe para Fundirla el Dia Domingo Fue Dia de
la Santa Cruz hamanecio Fundida el Dia martes se subio en la torecita.
Y se le pago el canpanero Dies pesos.y para q^e coste en todo tiempo la
Firme Dia sinco de Mayo*

Manuel Norberto Cruz y Serrano   *Son 10 p^s*

Martin Diego Cruz y Serrano

[fol. 25]

1791 haora Martes 3, de Mayo de 1791= me entrego el libro de
     mi Antesesor D^n Pedro de la Cruz Serrano. que Fue
     conquistador y fundador a mi Madrina Dª Marcela Dorotea
     y para que conste lo firme=

         Bernardino Antto de la + Serrano

1792 fue Gov.^{or} D^n Bernardino de la Cruz y Serrano

1795 otra bes oy en este año de 1795, años, salió por Gov^{or} D^n
     Bernardino de la Cruz y Serrano

*en el año de 1832 ha 15 de febrero rrexistro el organo D. Nasario
     Castillo se le pago 8 p^s y para q^e conste en todo tiempo la firmé
   Marin diego Cruz y Serrano   Manuel Serrano
<u>son 8 p^s</u>
en el año de 1835 ha 10 de setiembre el mismo se le pago 4 p^s por el
     organo por q^e se volbio ha descoponer y para q^e conste la firmé
     en la fecha y mes y año
   Martin diego Cruz y Serrano   Manuel Serrano
<u>son 4 p^s</u>*

[fol. 25v]

*Dia Miercoles ha 26 de õbre se habrio la puerta del coro de la capilla
     de la santisima Virgen de Guadalupe se le pagó al albanil tres
     rreales y medio*

1842

[fol. 27]

año de 1773 En este Pueblo de San Pablo Thepem . . . de la juridicion de Thenango del Valle en el año de mill setecientos setenta y 3 se comene[?] el corateral Mayor de esta Yglecia Parrochial siendo Gov.ᵒʳ D.ⁿ Antonio de los Santos alcalde ordinario D.ⁿ Alberto Fran.ᶜᵒ alcalde menor D.ⁿ Diego de la Cruz acarriando la madera a cuesta y travajo de todos los Naturales y tanvien dieron su limosna dhᵒˢ hijos para dhᵃ obra y para qᵉ coste lo firmo el ess.ⁿᵒ Fran.ᶜᵒ de la Cruz

Año de 1774 En dh.ᵒ año de mill setecientos setenta y cuatro actuo yo D.ⁿ Antonio de la Cruz de Gov.ᵒʳ deste dh.ᵒ pueblo alcalde Ordinario Dⁿ antonio Mathias alcalde Menor Dⁿ Fran.ᶜᵒ de la Cruz y en este año se cosecharon de trigo qᵉ salio de la comunidad del Pueblo para dhᵃ Obra treynta y dos cargas y se vendieron al precio de . . .
    se le entregaron a D.ⁿ Gillermo Serrano

[fol. 28]

Jesus Maria y Jose

Yo D.ⁿ Pedro de la Cruz Gov.ᵒʳ de tepemaxalco le pasé Señor Pascual Lopes esta tierra para que la sacamolee y la siembre algunos Años y asi que la dege la tomará el Señor Santo Santiago Apostol y mañana un otro dia Ninguno se la de quitar porque se la endono para que se allude quando se acuerde de alguna Cosa de Santa Yglecia yo la Doy en este Año de 1650 a.ˢ con los testigos Juan de Santiago jues Sebastian Serrano topile Baltesar Nicolas Miguel Xacobo Juan Costantino Antonion Matias Mateo Serrano todos estos testigos Aqui ponemos Nra firma Dⁿ Pedro de la Cruz Gov.ʳ yo Escribo por voluntad de Dⁿ Pedro de la Cruz Gov.ʳ felipe de la Cruz Es.ⁿᵒ Por mandado del Gov.ʳ de la Parcialidad de tepemaxalco D.ⁿ Bernardino de la Cruz y Serrano desendiente del Conquistador Dⁿ Pedro de la Cruz Serrano trasumpté esta Donasión del megicano a el Castillano a que me Remito la que esta sacada segun mi lial entender tepemaxalco y Abril 23 de 1795 y lo firme Basilio de Estrada testigos que se allaron presentes el alcalde actual Paulino Con toda su Rep. ᶜᵃ Regidor mayor Gervasio Paulino menor Juan Trinidad jues de [semtiera?] marselino Antonio Algualsil ?atiliano Anto Jose manuel topiles Pasados de dhᵃ Rep.ᶜᵃ

[fol. 28v]

de santiagito D.ⁿ Juan [?] D.ⁿ Pedro de Santiago y D.ⁿ tomas de
Aquino D.ⁿ Juan Antonio Dias Juan de Dios Rafel Antonio Fran.ᶜᵒ de
Salas Billegas Es.ⁿᵒ Pasado = y para que conste lo firme En dho dia
mes y año

Bern.ⁿᵒ Cruz y Serrano
Juez Gov.ʳ por su Mag.ᵈ

[fol. 29]

Oy dia Miercoles Henero onze de Mil ochocien . . . quatro amanecio
el dia Miercoles Nebando en la Cierra aqui Empeso a llobisnar,
como a las ocho del dia y toda la noche, llober y yober. el dia Jubes
en todo el dia hasta como despues de las doze de la noche Empezo
que amanecio de dia Biernes Empeso un ayre, fuerte que estubo
Resumbando el allire [for aire] en todo el Smo [for santisimo] dia
en dha Cierra hasta otra bes en la misma hora que Empeso que duro
beinte quatro Oras y aqui en este dho Monte tumbo palos, Em partes
y lugares como quien Echa rrastra, las que = no las pudo harrancar
las quebro, aqui en dho pueblo, algunas casas las destecho y algunas
casas las hamarraron con rriatas

[fol. 30]

Agosto 7 de 1809 años =

Se compuso la Organo de Nuebo de Ntra. Madre SSma de
Guadalupe, El Organista que conpuso, dho Organo D. Jose Peñalosas
llebo de su trabajo. quarenta y sinco quatro pesos. fuera de todos los
materiales que yo le di. que de el todo llego á secenta pesos. y para
que cosnte. lo firme en dho dia.

Bern.ⁿᵒ Cruz Y Zerrrano

[fol. 31]

tepem.ᶜᵒ febreᵒ de 12 aᵒ 1821

Se Empeso a desbaratar El Corerateral y Privisterio . . . dia siguiete se
acabo

[fol. 1]

1647

Now on the 6th of July 1647, concerning the church property, both the wind instruments and the organ, here let it be known that we managed it from scratch, Matías de San Francisco, *maestro*, and Pedro de la Cruz, organist. Here we will give offerings before God, beyond what has been given.

Juan de la Cruz: what he donates toward the organ is 110 pesos.

_____110 pesos

And Pedro de la Cruz, organist, donates 40 pesos.

_____ 40 pesos

Matías de San Francisco, maestro, donates 10 pesos.

_____ 10 pesos

Don Baltasar de los Reyes, gobernador, gives 50 pesos for the organ.

_____ 50 pesos

And the working men donated ten pesos.

_____ 10 pesos

Gabriel de San Pedro donates 20 pesos for the organ.

_____ 20 pesos

Juana Salomé, widow, donates 20 pesos for the organ.

_____ 20 pesos

Angelina Francisca donates 10 pesos.

_____ 10 pesos

Baltasar de Santiago donates five pesos.

_____5 pesos

Pedro Joaquín donates five pesos.

_____5 pesos

And the cantores gave 70 pesos. It came out of their tribute fields.

_____ 70 pesos

[fol. 1v]

And the people of San Lucas donated 10 pesos for the organ.

_____ 10 pesos

And another thirty pesos were added, with which I paid off a certain Christian individual

_____ 30 pesos

All together its price of 410 pesos was collected.

We who sign

Don Baltasar de los Reyes, gobernador

Don Juan de la Cruz	Pedro de la Cruz, organist
Matías Francisco, maestro	Gabriel de San Pedro
Juana Salomé	Angelina Francisca
Baltasar de Santiago	Pedro Joaquín

We all place our signatures. People are never to say that perhaps everybody bought the organ. Only a few people bought it.

[fol. 2]

1652

Now in the year 1652, only we tilled the soil of our tribute field at Topelaxtitlan:

Our father, Juan de la Cruz; and I, Pedro de la Cruz, organist; and Gabriel de San Pedro; and Francisco de la Cruz helped for a few days. No one is ever to say anywhere that perhaps the altepetl paid for the granary because only we five people bestirred ourselves. We helped for two years, and it was just our [maguey?]. We bestirred ourselves, my father, Juan de la Cruz, and I, Pedro de la Cruz, organist. In the year 1654 we harvested the corn that was sold. I went in by adding a 15-peso [figure of] holy San Juan, and with the fifteen pesos the colors were bought with which the church was painted. All together there were 30 pesos.

_____ 30 pesos

And then I helped with the dancing by having us buy breeches for twelve pesos and paying one peso and four reales to have them sewn up.

_____13 pesos, 4 reales

Witnesses: don Andrés de Santa María,	Pedro Hernández,
	juez major alcalde
Juan Martín, topile	Nicolás Pedro, escribano

1656

Now in the year 1656, concerning how the corncrib was built: People are never to say that perhaps the altepetl did it, for only we cantores bestirred ourselves. We built the corncrib. We spent two pesos, two reales, to pay the carpenters. Juan de la Cruz from San Antonio and Juan de San Miguel from Calimaya.

_____ 2 pesos, 2 reales

And I, Pedro de la Cruz, spent a peso to maintain the corncrib, together with Gabriel de San Pedro. People are never to say that perhaps the working men did it, because they only helped thatch it, and only a few hauled wood. Now holy San Juan's corn may be stored. Here I wrote it down on paper in the year 1657.

_____1 peso

[fol. 2v]

Before Francisco Hernández, alguacil mayor, and the cantores: Mateo Nicolás, topile, and the cantores, Nicolás Joseph, Diego Bernardo, Pedro Joaquín, Gabriel de San Francisco, and Diego Jacobo

1655

Now in the year 1655, on the 18th of October, concerning the land of San Francisco that was opened up [plowed]. People are never to say that perhaps everybody opened it up, because only a few people did the work. Here it will appear.

Teopanquiyahuac
Gabriel de Tapia: one yoke [of oxen]
Juan Bautista: one yoke
Jesús Nicolás: one yoke
Francisco Nicolás: two yokes
Pasiontitlan
Don Pedro de la Cruz, mayordomo of the holy church: five yokes
Don Juan de la Cruz, widow: one yoke
Pedro de Santiago: one yoke
Diego de la Cruz: two yokes
Diego Jacobo: one yoke
Tlatocapan
Juan Pablo: one yoke
Juan Mateo: one yoke Juan Moreno: one yoke
Francisco de la Cruz: seven yokes
Ventura de San Juan: one yoke
Pochtlan
Juan Martín, alguacil mayor, two yokes
Juan Bautista: one yoke
Matías de San Francisco: two yokes
Luis Damián: one yoke
Matías Francisco, alguacil mayor, one yoke
All together there were thirty-three yokes.

_____33 yokes [of oxen]

[fol. 3]

And the working men do not keep yokes [of oxen] for themselves. They just did a day's work, bringing a *huitzoctli* [pointed oak staff used to break sod]. Only a few people worked. People are never to say that perhaps everybody did. Don Pedro de la Cruz, mayordomo of the holy church, bestirred himself on behalf of the work. Don Diego de la Cruz, gobernador; and don Gabriel de San Pedro, alcalde; Sebastián Jacobo, *regidor mayor*; Juan de la Cruz, escribano. Now the work of don Pedro de la Cruz has been entered in the book.

1657

Now on Wednesday, the 10th of October 1657, here it is to be known how the land of San Francisco was opened up. It was the work of don Pedro de la Cruz, don Gabriel de San Pedro, alcalde; Sebastián Jacobo, regidor mayor; Melchior Cristóbal, regidor; Nicolás de San Pedro, escribano.

Teopanquiyahuac

Don Gabriel de San Pedro, alcalde	Juan Bautista, one yoke [of oxen]
Francisco Nicolás, one yoke	Francisco Jaime, one yoke
	Juan Mateo, one yoke

1658

Now in the year 1658, a bit more of San Francisco's land was opened up. It was the work of don Pedro de la Cruz, gobernador, [with] one yoke—Juan Moreno, one yoke—Juan Mateo, one yoke—Lucas Marcos, one yoke—and the working men do not keep yokes [of oxen] for themselves. They just brought *huitzoctli* staffs. People are never to say that perhaps everybody tilled the soil. It was the work of don Pedro de la Cruz, gobernador; don Gabriel de San Pedro, alcalde; Juan Francisco, regidor mayor; Juan Bautista, regidor; Luis Damián, *juez*. I did the writing, Nicolás de San Pedro, escribano. I place my signature; I am your work official.

[fol. 3v]

Now on Wednesday, the 10th of October 1658, perhaps it will be wondered at that the tribute field here at San Francisco was plowed. Indeed, it was my yoke of oxen and my say-so. A few working men tilled the land and placed maguey plants belonging to them. Four of the rows of magueys are my property, and I placed them there, don Pedro de la Cruz, gobernador. People are never to say that perhaps they are the property of the whole altepetl. I sorted out the question of whose property they are.

People were brought to swear. The witnesses will go into [the book]. Andrés de San Miguel, juez; Diego Jacobo; Juan Bautista; Juan Rafael; Nicolás Gaspar; Gabriel de San Francisco; Francisco Hernández; Melchior Cristóbal; don Diego de la Cruz, ex-gobernador; Francisco Nicolás; don Gabriel de San Pedro, alcalde. I did the writing, Nicolás de San Pedro, escribano.

Before all the witnesses of the working men and the women it was written down on this paper. The *cihuatepixqui* was Juana Hernández. Now in the year 1658, the corncrib was made higher. The cantores hauled the wood. The working men did not haul wood. People are never to say it is their property. Diego Jacobo, Andrés Nicolás, Juan Martín, and Bernabé Totonri [?] helped on the 16th of October. I gave Sebastián, the carpenter, two reales. It was his work. I did the writing, Nicolás de [San] Pedro, escribano.

Now in the year 1658, on the 14th of January, the *calvario* [small chapel] was rethatched. It was the work of don Pedro de la Cruz, gobernador.

1658

Now on Saturday, the 19th of January, the home of holy San Francisco [the chapel] was rethatched. And five *fanegas* of lime were bought. It was the work of don Pedro de la Cruz, gobernador.

The tribute house of San Francisco was put up. The working men of San Pablo Tepemaxalco put it up.

The people of San Lucas helped.

The people of Santa María de la Asunción helped. It was the work of don Pedro de la Cruz, gobernador.

[fol. 4]

Year	
1607	Now in the year 1607, the past gobernador don Buenaventura de Clemente died.
1608	
1609	
1610	Here don Francisco Martín became gobernador.
1611	Francisco Felipe was escribano.
1612	
1613	
1614	
1615	

1616   Here don Daniel Vázquez from San Antonio became gobernador.

1617

1618   Here a long comet appeared on the 10th of October, and there was a solar eclipse.

1619   Here the census taker, Cristóbal de Medranos, came to count people.

1620   The mayordomo [of the church] was Alejandro García.

1621

1622

1623

1624   Here don Juan Bautista became gobernador, and don Baltasar de los Reyes, alcalde.

1625   Here don Baltasar de los Reyes was made gobernador. There was an eclipse of the sun. It became dark as night.

1626

1627

1628

[fol. 4v]

1629   Now on the 26th of May, the crops froze and were totally destroyed.

1630   Here a census taker whose name was Almirante came to count people.

1631   Here don Matías Francisco became gobernador.

1632

1633

1634

1635   Now on the 24th of February, there came a great snow, on the day of San Matías the Apostle.

1636   On the 21st of June, the bridge at Atenco was set ablaze. We pushed it out [into the water?] over at San Francisco [on the San Francisco side?].

1637

1638

1639   There was a big earthquake.

1640

1641

1642   A strong epidemic began.

1643	On the 4th of August, on the day of Santo Domingo, the crops were lost as the ears of maize were forming.
1644	
1645	
1646	Now on Saturday, the 6th of January, our precious mother came out [on procession].
1647	Now on the 6th of March, we began the church of Santa María. The *guardián* Fray Baltasar died.
1648	
1649	
1650	Here [the chapel of] San Francisco was built.[32]
1651	On the 24th of February it [had] rained for a whole week.
[fol. 5]	
1652	
1653	Now in the year 1653, concerning how I painted the main altar: We gave offerings before God: I, Pedro de la Cruz; and Juan de la Cruz; and Francisco de Santiago. No one is ever to say that perhaps the altepetl did it, because only we gave the offering. We painted Santiago and the little choir and the lienzo of San Francisco. I, Pedro de la Cruz, donated 70 pesos.

_____ 70 pesos

And where the Santo Cristo was set up, I also did it, together with the sky. Eight pesos were spent.

_____ 8 pesos

And Juan de la Cruz donated twenty-three pesos.

_____23 pesos

And Francisco de Santiago donated 15 pesos.

_____ 15 pesos

And the church people painted the organ. They put down two reales. They helped, together with Matías de San Francisco. He gave 2 pesos and 4 reales.

_____ 2 pesos, 4 reales

And the one named Diego Bernardo gave five pesos.

_____5 pesos

32. Almost certainly the chapel of San Francisco is the church still standing now dubbed the Church of the Tercera Orden.

All together, there were 123 pesos and four reales.

_____123 pesos, 4 reales

First the father *guardián* placed his signature, then we placed our signatures.

Matías de San Francisco, maestro	Pedro de la Cruz, organist
Juan de la Cruz	Francisco de Santiago, together with the topiles
Francisco Hernández	Juan de San Miguel

1654   Now on Sunday, the 4th of January, the retablo of San Antonio was blessed.

1655   Here don Diego de la Cruz became gobernador. Now on Sunday, the 6th of June 1655, I began to paint. And when I, Pedro de la Cruz, finished, there was a painted arch inside the church. That's where the money went. Eight pesos were spent.

_____ 8 pesos

[fol. 5v]

1655   Here don Juan de la Cruz, my father, gave two pesos.

_____2 pesos

Then, in order to finish building the home for San Juan, I, Pedro de la Cruz, helped with 10 pesos.

_____ 10 pesos

I took fifteen pesos from the field dedicated to San Juan.

_____ 15 pesos

Fifteen pesos also came from his tribute fields.

_____ 15 pesos

In order that I, Pedro de la Cruz, could cover its being painted right away, all together there were 30 pesos.

_____ 30 pesos

Then it was painted. I alone took out that money, the fifteen pesos, so that the inside of the church could be painted.

_____ 15 pesos

Don Baltasar de los Reyes and Francisco de la Cruz topped it off with five pesos and two reales.

_____ 5 pesos, 2 reales

Then Lucas Marcos, a cantor, made an offering so that the colors with which the lienzo was painted were bought.

_____5 pesos

Before the rulers, I, Pedro de la Cruz, signed.

Don Diego de la Cruz, gobernador   Don Gabriel de San
Pedro, alcalde

Sebastián Jacobo, regidor mayor

Melchior Cristóbal, regidor; Matías de San Francisco,
maestro; Pedro Joaquín, alguacil mayor;
Juan de la Cruz, escribano

Right away on all the plots [little farms] all around the
macehualtin gave offerings. Someone would give two reales,
or someone four, or perhaps someone would give a peso. All
together they gave 95 pesos and two reales.

_____ 95 pesos, 2 reales

Another 25 pesos were spent in order to have the feast
of San Juan. People are not to say that maybe I spent all
of San Juan's money. My name is Pedro de la Cruz. I am
responsible for the home of San Juan as the mayordomo of
the holy church. The festival mass was done with 12 pesos.
Three fathers said mass, and we paid two pesos and four
reales for the wafers. It was the work of don Diego de la
Cruz, gobernador. Now on Monday, the 24th of July, in the
year 1655, I did the accounts for these people:

	Don Pedro Jacobo	Francisco Hernández
Diego Jacobo	Francisco Martín, fiscal	Andrés de San Miguel
Luis Damián	Andrés Nicolás	Juan Bautista

People are not to get upset.

1656   Here don Matías de San Francisco became gobernador.
[fol. 6]

1657   Here don Pedro de la Cruz himself became gobernador.

1658   For the second year don Pedro de la Cruz once again became
gobernador. Now on Sunday, the 19th of May, the bridge
was hauled in at Atenco. Now on Thursday, the 21st of
February, they jailed doña María de Mendoza.

1659   Don Pedro de la Cruz again became gobernador.
Now on Friday, the 3rd of January, at four o'clock, there
was a strong earthquake at the time of the ceremonies for
don Pedro de la Cruz, gobernador. On Saturday, the 4th
of January, there was another earthquake at one o'clock.
Now in the year 1659, I had been keeping the money of the
cantores so that they could cover the cost of some trumpets

and a guitar and a rebeck. All the money was spent. There is no more left of what I was keeping from the corn harvested in 1657, for which they got seven reales per fanega.

Now on Sunday, the 9th of February 1659, a breviary was purchased with six pesos of the corn money that helped feed them [the community members] in 1658. It was the work of Gabriel de Santiago, maestro; and don Pedro de la Cruz, gobernador.

_____ 6 pesos

Don Francisco Martín, alcalde. I did the writing, Juan Pablo, escribano.

And when the Santo Cristo was paid for, from that money I took one peso with which to buy oil.

_____1 peso

And ten reales also came out of it to buy sandals for the painter named Bernardo. All together seven pesos and two reales were spent. I was the one who wrote it, Juan Pablo, escribano.

_____ 7 pesos, 2 reales

And it seems the cantores took from the offering with which they covered the cost of the Santo Cristo a donation of three pesos and four reales.

_____ 3 pesos, 4 reales

Now in that very year 1659, three chests were bought, their price thirteen pesos, seven reales.

_____13 pesos, 7 reales

And six hats were bought then, their price four pesos, two reales.

_____ 4 pesos, 2 reales

And where did the money come from? We made real things come from clothing. [We sold clothing to buy things.] That is where the money came from.

Now on Saturday, the 28th of July, I gave seven pesos to the cantores; Francisco Hernández, maestro; and Diego Jacobo, alguacil mayor, with which they bought a big trumpet. It was my contribution, don Pedro de la Cruz, gobernador.

_____ 7 pesos

1660   Again don Pedro de la Cruz became gobernador.

Now on Thursday, the 22nd of April 1660, we paid three pesos and four reales for candles. They were needed for the Lenten procession [fol. 6v] of Santo Cristo. I do the writing for the cantores, Juan Pablo, maestro; Mateo Nicolás, topile.

_____ 3 pesos, 4 reales

Now on Thursday, the 24th of June 1660, we church people, the singers, give ten pesos for the Holy Cross. Our precious savior, who died on it for us sinners, may we revere him. No one is ever to say, "It was my money," because the cantores got it from the tribute maguey. And the working men put in four magueys. No one is ever to say anything. Here we place our signatures.

10 pesos

Don Pedro de la Cruz

Francisco Hernández, past *maestro* Mateo Nicolás, topile

　　　I did the writing, Juan Pablo, maestro

Before me, Felipe de la Cruz, escribano

And 15 pesos remain.

_____ 15 pesos

And Sr. don Pedro de la Cruz, gobernador, gave us two pesos to pay for masses and the *villancico* of San Pedro. It came from the corn. We brought the money, Francisco Hernández; Mateo Nicolás, topile; and I, Juan Pablo, maestro.

_____2 pesos

San Lucas

Now on Wednesday, the 19th of May 1660, at that point possession of the land in San Lucas was given to don Pedro de la Cruz, gobernador. He gave 10 pesos, and we gave it to Sr. the alcalde mayor, don Anastasio.

_____ 10 pesos

And the gobernador also gave one peso, four reales, to Juan de Aguilar, translator. He gave it to him.

_____ 1 peso, 4 reales

And the gobernador gave six hens, their price one peso, four reales.

_____ 1 peso, 4 reales

And he gave a dozen chickens, with which we entertained people from Metepec and Mexico [City].

_____ 1 peso, 4 reales
And he gave three reales, with which they placed the order
on leather [backing] and [got] a real's worth of flowers.

_____ 4 reales
And the gobernador gave three reales, with which cheese
was purchased, two reales' worth of vinegar and four of oil.
All together, it was nine reales.

_____ 9 reales
The gobernador gave another 10 tomines.

_____ 10 reales
And the gobernador gave one of his cloaks when we went to
Atenco. We got soaked inside the church on Friday. No one
took care of it until [fol. 7] Monday, when the gobernador
himself removed it and spread it outside. Then the pigs ate
it up on him, because at that time they grazed off the land
in the San Lucas plain. All together don Pedro de la Cruz,
gobernador, spent sixteen pesos, one real, plus one of his
cloaks.

_____ 16 pesos, 1 real

Don Pablo de Santiago, alcalde   don Cristóbal de San Gabriel,
                                     alcalde

   Francisco Martínez, juez

I did the writing, Felipe de la   I place my signature, Antonio
   Cruz, escribano   Joseph, escribano

Now Sunday, the first of August 1660, we bought three
granaries, their price twelve pesos and two reales. The
money came from the little tribute field San Juan has at
Pelaxtitlan. And one corncrib was purchased by Sr. don
Pedro de la Cruz, gobernador. It is his property. People are
never to say that maybe all three are his property.

_____ 12 pesos, 2 reales

1661   For the fifth year don Pedro de la Cruz again became
gobernador. At that time a lawsuit happened.
Now in the year 1661, the cantores' corn was harvested, nine
fanegas, sold for four pesos per carga.

_____ 9 fanegas

1662   Don Pedro de la Cruz again became gobernador for year six. He served for six months, and don Juan Pablo did another six months.

Now on Holy Wednesday, on the 5th of April 1662, a procession was held. We bought six pounds of candles, and we gave a peso to the father who held the procession. All together it was six pesos and two reales.

_____ 6 pesos, 2 reales

And I give four pesos to cover the cost of a trumpet.

_____ 4 pesos

And I gave two pesos so that paper could be bought. It came from the maguey.

_____2 pesos

And I gave fifteen pesos so that a base could be bought. The money came from the maguey.

_____ 15 pesos

Now in the year 1662 the cantores harvested 15 fanegas of corn.

_____ 15 fanegas

[fol. 8]

1663   Don Pedro de la Cruz became gobernador for year seven. The lawsuit calmed down. On Holy Thursday there was a big frost, and the stars were blotted out again.

Now on Holy Wednesday, the 21st of March 1663, there was a procession. Six pounds of candles were brought, and a peso was given to the father who led the procession. All together it was six pesos and two reales.

6 pesos, 2 reales

Now in the year 1663, the cantores harvested their corn:
[space left blank]

1664   Don Pedro de la Cruz became gobernador for year eight. Now on Monday, the 15th of September 1664, here let it be known, concerning the carpenter named Baltasar Pascual, maestro, that he made the side altarpiece of our precious mother, Santa María de la Asunción, for the pay of 25 pesos. The money was the gobernador's property.

_____25 pesos

And the gobernador gave another three pesos, likewise of his own property.

_____3 pesos

And the gobernador don Pedro de la Cruz gave fifteen pesos of his money in order that the side altarpiece be paid for.

_____15 pesos

Then the side altarpiece was consecrated. The gobernador don Pedro de la Cruz spent seventeen pesos.

_____17 pesos

Four pounds of [regular] candles and two pounds of taper candles, their price all together four pesos and one real. The money was also the property of the gobernador, don Pedro de la Cruz.

_____ 4 pesos, 1 real

The paint and the whitewash and the glue and the painter's pay all together were ten pesos. The money was also the property of the gobernador, don Pedro de la Cruz.

_____ 10 pesos

And he gave three cargas of lime, its price three pesos. The money was also the property of don Pedro de la Cruz.

_____3 pesos

Then a litter was purchased. The gobernador gave five pesos of his own property.

_____5 pesos

And he gave a bell, its price thirty-five pesos. The money was also the property of don Pedro de la Cruz, gobernador.

_____35 pesos

And an *arroba* of wine was purchased, its price six pesos. It was also the gobernador who bought it.

_____ 6 pesos

[fol. 8v]

All together the gobernador don Pedro de la Cruz gave 120 pesos to Santa María de la Asunción. People are not to get upset. His children and grandchildren are not to dishonor the agreement. Now in the year 1666, don Pedro de la Cruz was in the tenth year of his governorship. I did the writing, Antonio Joseph, escribano.

_____120 pesos

1665   Once again don Pedro de la Cruz was established.

Now on Sunday, October 2nd, 1665, the church and the side
altarpiece of our precious revered mother were consecrated.
There were two days of bullfights. We officials looked on.

Don Pedro de la Cruz, gobernador

| Don Matías Francisco, | Juan Bautista, | Don Pedro Hernández, |
| alcalde | alcalde | alcalde |

Juan Martín, juez mayor   Miguel Serrano, fiscal

Antonio Joseph, escribano

And the people of Santa María did not put down any
money. Just a certain amount with which they held the
fiesta, 21 pesos, for that they looked on.

_____ 21 pesos

And the price of the ropes they sold was sixty pesos. Don
Baltasar de los Reyes, past gobernador, went to leave them.

_____ 60 pesos

And a litter was purchased for thirty-five pesos. It was
the money of the cofradía of our precious revered mother,
the mayordomo being Miguel Serrano. I did the writing,
Antonio Joseph, escribano.

_____ 35 pesos

[fol. 9]

1666   Now in the year 1666, don Pedro de la Cruz again became
gobernador.

Now on Saturday, the 7th of March, I bought a trumpet for
the cantores, its price fifteen pesos. The money came from
the pared-off maguey. Lorenzo López was the maestro [of
the church] and Francisco Jaime alguacil mayor. It was the
work of don Pedro de la Cruz. I did the writing, Antonio
Joseph, escribano.

_____ 15 pesos

And Sr. don Pedro de la Cruz donated four pesos and two
reales of his own money.

_____ 4 pesos, 2 reales

Now on Thursday, the 2nd of February 1666, we made an
account of the cantores' money in front of everybody, one
hundred and seventy pesos. People are not to get upset.
Here we let it be known. It was the work of Sr. don Pedro de
la Cruz. I did the writing, Felipe de la Cruz, escribano.

_____ 170 pesos

And a trumpet and glasses and paper were bought with forty pesos.

_____ 40 pesos

Now in the year 1666, we, the cantores, put in 100 pesos to buy the organ. The money came from the maguey.

_____ 100 pesos

We signed in front of one another when the account was done. Don Francisco Martín, fiscal

The respected Sr. don Pedro de la Cruz, gobernador, brought forth his money before God to pay for the organ. He gave 100 pesos before us cantores. My name is Lorenzo López, maestro, and I sign.

Diego Bernardo, alguacil mayor; Gaspar Melchior, past alguacil mayor; Francisco Jaime, past alguacil mayor; Diego Jacobo, alguacil mayor; Diego Serrano, topile; Gabriel de San Francisco, topile. I did the writing, Antonio Joseph, escribano. Don Matías Francisco, alcalde; don Juan Martín, alcalde; Felipe de la Cruz, escribano.

[fol. 9v]

Now in the year 1666, here in San Pablo Tlatocapan Ahuatitlan, here let it be known, concerning the organ, that Sr. don Pedro de la Cruz, gobernador, has donated four hundred pesos, and the cantores, one hundred. They have given all together five hundred pesos, the price [of the organ]. Here let it be known. It was consecrated on March 19, the feast day of San Joseph.

_____ 500 pesos

Don Matías de San Francisco, alcalde   Don Juan Miguel, alcalde

Don Antonio Juárez, alcalde   Don Gabriel de San Pedro,
                                         alcalde

Francisco Matías, alguacil mayor   Luis Damián, mayordomo
Francisco Hernández, regidor mayor

I did the writing, Felipe de la Cruz, escribano

1667   Now in the year 1667, don Pedro de la Cruz again became gobernador.

Now in the year 1667, the door was blessed and some things for the main church of the convento, on the day of the holy sacrament, the 9th of June. The money did not come from

the community. It was the gobernador, señor don Pedro
de la Cruz, who donated it before God, eighty pesos, with
which the stone masons and the carpenters were paid.
People are never to say that maybe the money came from
the community or the people of the altepetl.

_____ 80 pesos

And the people of Calimaya gave no money. They just fed
people, and the gobernador fed both the master named
Roque Flores and the one named Juan Blas. The gobernador
spent twelve pesos on the food.

_____ 12 pesos

It was the work of don Pedro de la Cruz, gobernador; don
Matías de San Francisco, alcalde; don Pablo de Santiago,
alcalde; Gabriel de Tapia, regidor mayor; Juan Alonso,
regidor; Andrés Nicolás, juez. I did the writing, Felipe de la
Cruz, escribano. There were all together ninety-two pesos.
Here let it be known.

_____ 92 pesos

[fol. 10]

And we also put a new metal foot-plate on the door to
the sacristy, its price two pesos, together with a knocker,
its price, three pesos and four reales. It was also Sr. the
gobernador who donated it.

_____ 5 pesos 4 reales

1668   Now in the year 1668, don Pedro de la Cruz again became
gobernador.

Here let it be known that Sr. don Pedro de la Cruz,
gobernador, donated to the church the clothing for our
precious revered mother, together with the [cost of the]
cupola, including the lime that was bought [to paint it
white] and the angel [painted] on the cupola that was put up
and the mazaris [tile-shaped bricks used to build it] and the
pay of the carpenters. All together he spent 187 pesos and
four reales. Here let it be known.

187 pesos, 4 reales

And a Jesús Nazareno, its price fifty pesos.

_____ [blank]

And his ornaments

_____ [blank]

And one lamp, its price 120 pesos, belonging to Jesús
Nazareno. *It contains eleven marks, three ounces of silver. The
plate with which wages and offerings are collected has three
marks, four ounces of silver, and [also] belongs to the Jesús
Nazareno.*

_____120 pesos

And the stand for our mother of Asunción, and the pay of
the carpenter and the painter, all together was sixty pesos.

_____ 60 pesos

[fol. 11]

1669 Now in the year 1669, don Pedro de la Cruz again became
gobernador, and don Francisco Martín, alcalde.
Now here let it be known, concerning the side altarpiece
of our precious revered mother of Asunción: Her side
altarpiece was consecrated and went into the main church.
Everything, the image and the pay of the carpenters and,
at the time of the blessing, the candles purchased and the
gunpowder [for fireworks] and the roan horses, all together
cost 300 pesos. The consecration was on February 24, the
day of San Matías the Apostle. It was the gobernador don
Pedro de la Cruz who donated it [all].

_____ 300 pesos

Before the alcaldes

Don Francisco Martín, don Nicolás Gaspar, don Antonio Juárez,
     alcalde   alcalde   alcalde

I did the writing, Felipe de la Cruz, escribano.
Now on Thursday, the 21st of March 1669, here it will be
known that the one called little Josepha, whom we raised,
who was raised in our home, today married the one called
Diego de Santiago.

1670 Now in the year 1670, don Pedro de la Cruz again became
gobernador and Juan Martín, alcalde.

1671 Now in the year 1671, don Matías de San Francisco became
gobernador, and don Pablo de San Juan and don Gabriel de
Tapia, the alcaldes.

[fol. 11v]

Year

1672 Now in the year 1672, don Pedro de la Cruz again became
gobernador. The alcaldes were don Juan Martín, don

Francisco Hernández, don Miguel Serrano, and Felipe de
la Cruz, escribano. In 1672 a census taker came to count
people. Don Diego de Guidos from Guadalajara, alcalde
mayor, was the census taker. The secretary don Pedro
[illegible] de Novo did it. Francisco de la Cruz was the
translator.

All of us people of Asunción were put into the register.

1673   Now in the year 1673, don Pedro de la Cruz again became
gobernador. The alcalde was don Juan Martín. Now in the
year 1673 a monument for Holy Week was needed. The
gobernador don Pedro de la Cruz donated 55 pesos toward
its price.

_____55 pesos

Now on Saturday, the 22nd of July 1673, don Pedro de la
Cruz, gobernador, donated an organ to the main church of
the friary, its price 650 pesos.

_____ 650 pesos

And the gobernador also donated the door of the chapel, its
price forty pesos, in the year 1674.

_____ 40 pesos

And the cost for [renting] the roan horses, two pesos.

_____2 pesos

[fol. 12]

1674   Now in the year 1674, don Pedro de la Cruz again became
gobernador. The alcaldes were don Juan Martín, don Miguel
Serrano, and don Juan Diego. Now on the 25th of August
1674, the door of San Juan's home was put in place, its price
50 pesos. It was made in Mexico City, paid for with San
Juan's money. It was observed and done before the officials.
Don Pedro de la Cruz, gobernador, took care of it.

_____ 50 pesos

Also the lock
And the churchly home of holy San Francisco was fixed
up in the year 1674. Sr. don Pedro de la Cruz, gobernador,
donated forty pesos.

_____ 40 pesos

The mules of the gobernador don Pedro de la Cruz worked
to transport the sand and mud, and he paid those who

worked. No one bestirred themselves. He alone took care of it.

~~Now Sunday the 15th~~

Now Sunday, the 15th of September 1678, here let it be known that the people of Santa María de la Asunción came to give 280 pesos, before don Juan Martín, gobernador.
Don Nicolás Blas, alcalde Don Miguel Serrano, alcalde
Don Andrés García, past alcalde Don Antonio Juárez, past fiscal
Francisco Diego, regidor mayor
I did the writing, Lorenzo de Santiago, escribano
I, don Juan de la Cruz, alcalde, received the money
280 pesos
[fol. 12v]
Now Sunday, the 15th of September 1678, here let it be known that the people of Santa María de la Asunción have come to deliver 40 pesos. I receive the money, don Juan de la Cruz, alcalde, before all the rulers.

40 pesos

Don Juan Martín, gobernador	Don Nicolás Blas, alcalde	Don Miguel Serrano, alcalde
Don Andrés García, past alcalde		Don Antonio Juárez, past fiscal
	Francisco Diego, regidor mayor	

Lorenzo de Santiago, escribano
[fol. 13]
Here let it be known: in the year 1677, on the 2nd day of the month of June, on Friday, the holy feast day of San Juan, I was attacked. I was tripped. They really beat me up, don Juan de la Cruz, *alcalde ordinario*. Here it will appear. At the same time, things [problems] started for my late mother-in-law, doña Ana Juana, also right on the holy feast day of San Juan Bautista. She did nothing for a week. She died on Wednesday, and on Thursday we buried her, I and my wife doña Josepha de la Cruz. Here it will appear.

And here let it be known: I went to Toluca. I got better, then I got
worse again. So I was in Toluca for a long time when I went
to inform [the authorities of what had happened]. At the
same time [while I was gone], my brothers-in-law Mateo
Juárez and Felipe de la Cruz both died, as well as one of my
sisters, Catarina. And afterward my late beloved mother
died, María Salomé. It all happened in that same year. Here
let it be known; here it will appear.

Also in the year 1677 my compadre don Lorenzo López, past maestro
[de capilla], was disgraced. Francisco de la Cruz, alcalde,
disgraced him. He arrested him on the road at night at a
little after seven o'clock. He disgraced my compadre, who is
imprisoned at Metepec. Here it will appear.

And here it will appear: when the choir of cantores were about to
play [their wind instruments] as soon as the candles were
lit, when the people of the altepetl of San Pedro [Calimaya]
and San Pablo [Tepemaxalco] were gathering, that one,
alcalde Francisco [de la Cruz], who mumbles, was speaking
calumnies. I bestirred myself to address the *guardián*, Fray
Juan Bautista, a week later, when we cantores held a fiesta
here in Tepemaxalco. It all happened here in the year it was
written, 1677.

1679   Here let it be known that when the church canopy was
purchased in the year 1679, it was discussed and asked for.
130 pesos were given. It came from the money from San
Francisco's tribute corn, which was sold for sixty pesos. The
tribute maguey brought twenty pesos. Doña Clara Leonor
took care of the tribute maguey, together with Nicolás
Francisco. And I, don Juan de la Cruz, past alcalde, offered
fifty pesos when we brought [the canopy] on the 15th of
September. It was taken out for the first time at dawn. Here
it will appear. People are not to say anything.

And here I place it before them. We will be witnesses
tomorrow and forever. If anyone says anything, those who
speak will leave all to God and his precious mother, the
Lady Santa María.

Don Pedro de Santiago, past alcalde Don Ambrosio de San
Juan, past alcalde

Don Lorenzo López, *maestro de capilla* Diego Felipe, mayordomo

Melchior FranciscoMarcos de Santiago Lucas de San Juan

[15v]

Memo concerning the dead person, the old man Sebastián Jacobo, and what was spent when he died.

Here let it be known, in the year 1668: a shroud, its price 12 pesos.	12 pesos
A fanega of corn was needed, its price one peso and four reales.	1 peso, 4 reales
One pound of candles, seven reales.	7 reales
We gave one lamb, its price six reales.	6 reales
All together fifteen pesos and one real were spent.	15 pesos, 1 real

I, Josepha Francisca, shrouded him. He left me a piece of land on the road to San Lucas, at the edge of the wood, where the grassland is. No one is ever to say anything about it, because Sebastián Jacobo was my grandfather. It was the contribution of my beloved father, don Pedro de la Cruz, gobernador. Don Gabriel de San Pedro, alcalde San Lucas alcalde, don Pablo de San Juan

I did the writing, don Nicolás de San Pedro, past escribano.

[fol. 16]

Now on Thursday, the 19th of March 1682, at three o'clock there was a strong earthquake. It lasted a half hour before it ended, right on the feast day of the holy San Joseph, in the time of Sr. don Simón being alcalde mayor, Fray Juan Bautista, *guardián*; and don Pedro Rodríguez, secretario. Here in San Pablo Tepemaxalco, let it be known in this book. It is the work of don Juan de la Cruz, gobernador, and don Lorenzo López, alcalde ordinario.

Don Nicolás Blas, alcalde of San Lucas   Don Antonio Juárez, alcalde of Asunción Don Sebastián Serrano, alcalde of Santiago   Francisco Nicolás, regidor mayor

Don Andrés de Santiago, escribano público

[fol. 16v]

Now on Wednesday, the 31st of March 1683, here in San Pablo Tepemaxalco, in [the tlaxilacalli of] Tlatocapan, here we place signatures. My name is don Francisco Nicolás, past

alcalde. My wife is Teresa Francisca. Before God I say, by
means of my will: with all my heart I leave one plot of land
to my precious revered mother, our Lady of Guadalupe,
whose precious revered son is Jesús Nazareno. There her
magueys will be planted. No one is ever to say anything,
for I give it of my own free will. Now at my time of death I
give ten magueys. We enter them into the holy cofradía, I
and my wife and one dependent named Josepha. Before all
the rulers, I place my signature. My name is don Francisco
Nicolás, past alcalde. She is Teresa Francisca.
We are keepers of the altepetl by our lord God.

Don Juan de la Cruz, gobernador	Don Lorenzo López, alcalde ordinario
Don Diego Gonzales, fiscal mayor	Señora Ayala Gonzales, Spanish witness

I do the writing on behalf of the sick man—don Andrés de Santiago,
escribano

[fol. 17]

Now on Wednesday, the 3rd of February 1683, here in San Pablo
Tepemaxalco [in the tlaxilacalli of] Ahuatitlan Tlatocapan,
here let it be known in this book everything needed for
the retablo of the holy sacraments and holy San Pedro
and San Pablo so that they will be painted. Here will
appear whatever is spent. The *macehualtin* are never to
say anything. We will let it be known in this book, we
the keepers of the altepetl by our lord God: don Juan de
la Cruz, gobernador; don Lorenzo López, alcalde; don
Agustín Diego, alcalde; don Nicolás Blas, alcalde; don
Miguel Serrano, alcalde; don Sebastián Serrano, alcalde;
don Diego González, fiscal; don Tomás de la Cruz, regidor
mayor; Antonio de los Santos, regidor; Nicolás Francisco,
mayordomo. I do the writing, don Andrés de Santiago.

When we went to Mexico City, we picked up the gold that Sr.
Conde de Santiago gave us: three hundred pounds of gold.
We divided it with the people of Calimaya. They took 150
pounds, and likewise we of Tepemaxalco took 150 pounds.

And we bought three pounds of Spanish *bol* [used by gilders],
its price four pesos, 4 reales. The money came from the
community. Here it will appear.

_____ 4 pesos, 4 reales
And we bought three pesos worth of glue.

_____ 3 pesos
[fol. 17v]
And we bought four pounds of transparent gypsum, its price one peso, four reales.

_____ 1 peso, 4 reales
We are the ones who went to Mexico City: don Juan de la Cruz, gobernador; don Lorenzo López, alcalde; don Nicolás Blas, alcalde; don Sebastián Serrano, alcalde. Three pesos and four reales were spent in Mexico on food for the rulers.

_____ 3 pesos, 4 reales
Now on Saturday, the 13th of February 1683, Sr. Don Diego Castillo, master painter, began to work. I alone donated three weeks' worth of food for him, I, don Juan de la Cruz, gobernador, with doña Josepha Francisca, *gobernadora*. None of the *macehualtin* are ever to say anything.
Now on Tuesday, the 2nd of March, don Nicolás Blas, the alcalde of San Lucas, went to Mexico to buy whatever was needed by the master painters [for their dinners]. Here it will appear.

A half an arroba of sugar was purchased, its price three pesos and two reales.

_____ 3 pesos, 2 reales
And four pounds of cocoa beans, the price

_____ 2 pesos, 4 reales
Four reales' worth of cinnamon

_____ 4 reales
Robalo fish, the price

_____ 2 pesos, 4 reales
A half an arroba of shrimp, the price

_____ 2 pesos, 4 reales
And two pesos, four reales' worth of lentils

_____ 2 pesos, 4 reales
[fol. 18]
And one peso's worth of beans

_____ 1 peso
And six reales' worth of saffron

_____ 6 reales

Two reales' worth of peppers

_____ 2 reales

Two quarts of Castillian oil, the price

_____1 peso

Two reales' worth of olives

_____ 2 reales

Two reales' worth of vinegar

_____ 2 reales

One real's worth of garlic

_____ 1 real

Now on Friday, the 18th of March 1683, we put together all the bills
    that we paid to Sr. don Diego Castillo, master painter. We
    gave him 120 pesos. Here it will appear. No tribute was
    imposed; it came from the whole community. No one is ever
    to say anything about it.

_____120 pesos

And to Sr. Miguel de Blancas [the other craftsman], we also gave 120
pesos.

_____120 pesos

And Sr. Don Juan de la Cruz, gobernador, and doña Josepha
    Francisca, *gobernadora*, donated and brought the eighty
    pesos.

_____ 80 pesos

And in order that holy San Pablo be dressed, dyes were purchased
    through an agreement made elsewhere. It was done for
    seven pesos.

_____ 7 pesos

[fol. 18v]

And we here in Tepemaxalco are responsible for cleaning the Santo
    Cristo from the middle and above, for the cost of eight
    pesos.[33]

_____ 8 pesos

And in order that both San Bernardino and Santa Clara in the
tabernacle be cleaned, six pesos.

_____ 6 pesos.

33. Jim Lockhart's theory was that the people of Calimaya were probably responsible for cleaning the bottom half of the statue, and the people of Tepemaxalco the
upper half.

And to Tomás the craftsman, for gilding, we gave seven pesos.

_____ 7 pesos

And to Francisco de la Cruz we gave 5 pesos.

_____5 pesos

And [papier-mâché] flesh so that the angels could have flesh put
    on, the price two pesos and six reales. Here it will appear. It
    came from the community.

_____ 2 pesos, 6 reales

[fol. 19]

The lamps of the parish were weighed: Jesús and San Juan, 58 marks,
    which were given by donation on October 2, 1810.Maya

[fol. 21]

In the year 1733 and in the year 1734, don Nicolás de la Cruz became
gobernador.

And in the year 1743, don Nicolás de la Cruz became gobernador.

Here in this year of 1745, don Nicolás de la Cruz became gobernador
    again. And here will appear, here we state clearly, the
    expenses of having a new Saint of Jerusalem[34] made. It cost
    20 pesos. Here will appear what was given in support: the
    children of holy San Lucas supported it with one peso.

_____1 peso

[fol. 21v]

The children of Santa María de la Asunción, the alcaldes, supported
it with one peso1 peso The children of holy Santiago the Apostle, the
alcaldes, supported it with one peso _____1 peso

The children of holy San Francisco Puxtlan supported it with one
peso; here it will appear_____1 peso

And here in our altepetl of holy San Pablo Tepemaxalaco Tlatocapan
Ahuatitlan, the *cabecera* [leading community], we put down sixteen
pesos _____16 pesos

And let it be known everywhere that the shirt belongs to the Saint of
Jerusalem.

---

34. In theory the "new Saint of Jerusalem" could refer in some indirect way to a
model of Holy Jerusalem [the city], but a little further down they mention "his shirt,"
so they are talking about a saint. Since there is no known Saint of Jerusalem, they are
most likely referring to Jesus himself.

We say clearly that the holy San Felipe and Santiago came [and
was finished up?] and was paid for through their children's
wooded land. Four pesos were taken for his shirt.

[fol. 23v] [Spanish translation of facing page, fol. 24, with signature
of Manuel de la Cruz y Serrano running down the side margin]

[top line torn off] *the bells of the chapel of the most holy Virgin of
Guadalupe, that were recast. My great-great-grandfather did
it, don Nicolás de la Cruz y Serrano.*

*Today, Wednesday, the 9th of March 1746, the recasting of the bells of
our Lady of Guadalupe was completed at dawn. In this barrio
of San Pablo Tepemaxalco, I, the mayordomo, don Nicolás de
la Cruz, am the present gobernador, and here begins the list of
expenses that appear:*

*I bought one arroba [25-pound unit] and three pounds of metal for 5
pesos*   *5 pesos*

And another arroba ....3 pesos, 1 real

*And three pounds of tin [imported?], two pesos, one-and-a-half reales
....2 pesos, 1.5 reales*

And I fed the bell maker, two pesos and half a real ....2 pesos, 0.5 real

*And for when we had the blessing, three pesos, two reales ....3 pesos, 2
reales*

And I also cast another medium-sized bell. I gave 22 pesos....... 22 pesos

*And I paid 35 pesos for the two bells I had made new, to maestro don
Miguel Alvarez..35 pesos*

What the sum total adds up to is 72 pesos, 6 reales ..... 72 pesos, 6 reales

*And I say that I, don Nicolás de la Cruz, together with my nephews,
Francisco de la Cruz and Antonio de la Cruz, collected and
worked for the funds with which we paid for the bells. Don
Ambrosio de la Cruz gave an offering of three reales, and don
Clemente gave four reales. And I copied this today, November
10, 1842.*

[fol. 24]

Today, Wednesday, the 9th of March 1746, the recasting of the bells
of our Lady of Guadalupe was completed at dawn. In this
barrio of San Pablo Tepemaxalco, I, the mayordomo, don
Nicolás de la Cruz, am the present gobernador, and here
begins the list of expenses that appear:

I bought one arroba and three pounds of metal for 5 pesos......5 pesos

And another arroba, its price three pesos, one real .... 3 pesos, 1 real

And five pounds of tin that cost two pesos, one-and-a-half reales
.... 2 pesos, 1.5 reales
And I maintained the bell maker, two pesos and half a real
....2 pesos, 0.5 real
And for when we had the blessing, three pesos, two reales
....3 pesos, 2 reales
And I also widened another medium-sized bell. I gave for the
enlargement 22 pesos..22 pesos
And I paid for the two bells I had made new, 35 pesos to maestro
        named Miguel Alvarez   35 pesos
[fol. 24v]
What the sum total of my expenses adds up to is 72 pesos, 6 reales
There are: 72 pesos, 6 reales
And I say that I, don Nicolás de la Cruz, together with my nephews,
        Francisco de la Cruz and Antonio de la Cruz, collected and
        worked for the funds with which we paid for the bells.
Don Ambrosio de la Cruz gave an offering of three reales3 reales
Don Lucas Clemente gave an offering of four reales4 reales [The
following is in Spanish in the same hand as the translation on fol.
23v.]

*On the 25th of March, in the year 1829, the little bell of the chapel of
the most holy mother Guadalupe was taken down to be recast.
It was at dawn on Sunday, the day of the Holy Cross. It was
cast on Tuesday and brought up to the little tower. Ten pesos
were paid to the bell maker. So that it may be verified for all
time, I have signed on the 5th day of May.*

        Manuel Norberto Cruz y Serrano   10 pesos
        Martín Diego Cruz y Serrano
[fol. 25]
1791. Now on March 3, 1791, I deliver the book of my ancestor, don
        Pedro de la Cruz y Serrano, founder and conqueror, to my
        godmother, doña Marcela Dorotea, and to attest it I sign
        Bernardino Antonio de la Cruz y Serrano
1792. Don Bernardino de la Cruz y Serrano was gobernador.
1795. Again in the year of 1795, don Bernardino de la Cruz y Serrano
turned out to be gobernador.

In the year 1832, on the 15th of February, don Nasario Castillo tuned
the organ. He was paid eight pesos, and to attest it I have
signed
Martín Diego Cruz y Serrano   Manuel Serrano

8 pesos

In the year 1835, on September 10, the same man was paid four pesos
for the organ, because it had
broken again, and to attest it I sign on the date and month and year
Martín Diego Cruz y Serrano   Manuel Serrano

4 pesos
[fol. 25v]
On Wednesday, the 26th of October, the door was opened to the
chapel choir [loft] of the most holy Virgin of Guadalupe. The
carpenter was paid three-and-a-half reales.
1842

[fol. 27]
Year 1773 In this pueblo of San Pablo Tepemaxalco, in the
jurisdiction of Tenango del Valle, in the year of 1773, [was
repaired?] the main side altar of this parish church when
don Antonio de los Santos was gobernador; don Alberto
Francisco, alcalde ordinario; don Diego de la Cruz, *alcalde
menor*, carrying back the wood with the effort and work of
all the local people and the said children [of the land] also
gave their offering for the said work, and to attest it I sign
Francisco de la Cruz, notary
Year 1774 In this year of 1774, I, don Antonio de la Cruz, act as
gobernador of this pueblo; alcalde ordinario don Antonio
Matías; *alcalde menor* don Francisco de la Cruz, and in this
year thirty-two cargas of wheat from the community of the
pueblo were harvested for this work, and they were sold at
the price of: [*left blank*]
They [the funds] were given to don Guillermo Serrano.

[fol. 28]

Jesus, Mary, and Joseph

I, don Pedro de la Cruz, gobernador of Tepemaxalco [have passed? or lent?] to señor Pascual López this land to break and sow for a few years, and when he leaves it, the lord Santo Santiago the Apostle will get it, and from tomorrow onward nobody is to take it away from him, since I donated it so that he may be supported whenever anyone remembers the connection to the holy church. I give it in this year of 1650 before witnesses Juan de Santiago, juez; Sebastián Serrano, topile; Baltasar Nicolás; Miguel Jacobo; Juan Constantino; Antonio Matías; Mateo Serrano, before all these witnesses here we place our signature. Don Pedro de la Cruz, gobernador. I write on behalf of don Pedro de la Cruz, gobernador; Felipe de la Cruz, notary. By the order of the gobernador of the subaltepetl of Tepemaxalco, don Bernardino de la Cruz y Serrano, descendant of the conquistador don Pedro de la Cruz y Serrano, I translated this donation from Nahuatl to Spanish, and I confirm that it is done according to my fair understanding, Tepemaxalco, 23rd of April 1795, and I signed it, Basilio de Estrada. Witnesses who were present: the present alcalde Paulino with all his *república* [meaning community], regidor mayor Gervasio Paulino, [regidor] menor Juan Trinidad, juez of [?] Marcelino Antonio, alguaciles Antonio, José Manuel, past topiles of said *república*.

[fol. 28v]

from Santiaguito[?], don Juan [?], don Pedro de Santiago and don Tomás de Aquino, don Juan Antonio Díaz, Juan de Dios, Rafael Antonio, Francisco de Salas Villegas, past notary == and to attest it I signed it in said day, month, and year

Bernardino Cruz y Serrano
Juez Gobernador for His
Majesty

[fol. 29]

Today, Wednesday, the 11th of January 1804, it was snowing at the break of the day on the mountain. Here it started to drizzle, around 8:00 a.m. and for the whole night, raining and raining on Thursday all day until after midnight. At dawn on Friday a strong wind started; it made the air buzz for the whole day on the said mountain until the same hour it had started. It lasted twenty-four hours, and here on the said mountain it knocked down trees in various places, like someone flattening the ground [before sowing], and it broke off those that it could not pull out, and in the said pueblo it took the roof off some houses, while other houses were tied down with ropes.

[fol. 30]
7th [of] August 1809 =
The organ of Nuestra Madre Santísima de Guadalupe was repaired again. The organist who repaired the said organ, don José Peñalosas, charged for his work forty-five pesos, on top of all the materials that I gave him, so for all it was sixty pesos, and to attest it I signed it on this day.

Bernardino Cruz y Serrano

[fol. 31]
Tepemaxalco, 12th [of] February 1821
The side altar and the presbytery started to break and on the next day it broke apart.

When don Pedro de la Cruz was elected gobernador in 1657, he began to keep a tribute record book. It is understandable that he believed this was necessary, as across Mexico indigenous elected officials could find themselves being carted off to jail if they failed to produce the required tribute or if their own people accused them of corruption (that is, of siphoning off some of the money). Sadly, over the years the first page or two of the record was loosened and eventually fell off and was lost. Thus, we offer the record for 1658, the first year that the whole tribute collection is visible.

Every adult owed three tostones, or half pesos, for a total of 1.5 pesos. Thus, a widow or unmarried adult owed three tostones, and a married couple (represented by the male head of household) owed six. In other records from other regions, it is clear that people sometimes tried to pass off their adolescent children as younger than they really were to avoid the payment of an additional three tostones when they reached maturity, but, eventually, they would admit that the child had become an adult. This was generally shortly before the young person was married in any case.

In some ways the system was fair in that, in this region, everybody paid; there was no exception made for the nobility. On the other hand, the weight of such a payment would have been felt as much greater by a poor man than by someone like don Pedro. Likewise, when a married person was widowed, the law was merciful in that it was understood that the household tribute should immediately drop to three tostones, even if the farm's income remained more or less the same; the lost labor *would be painful enough in other regards. Yet this record shows that, occasionally, a woman head of household was in fact charged the full six tostones. Why might this have been? Perhaps such women lived with grown sons or invalid husbands, or maybe their husbands had absconded, their whereabouts unknown.*

In one part of the book, don Pedro carefully listed every tribute payer in each tlaxilacalli so that there was a way of calculating how much was owed. In another part of the book, he recorded the payments made by village officials. He wanted the people to feel satisfied that he was accurately recording the amount of money they had paid, and most of them could not read, so he followed an ancient pictoglyphic system, using a different symbol to represent each element of tribute, as had been done for generations before the conquest. He used one kind of mark to represent a peso, and another mark to represent a tomín, which was a coin in common circulation that represented one-eighth of a peso. Counting carefully, we see that, normally, the visual record and the alphabetic record do agree. Only in the case of a tlaxilacalli that paid months late is there a discrepancy. Perhaps they owed a fine that everyone present understood and so is not recorded. It is unlikely that don Pedro was trying to cheat them. It is clear that the barrios were rarely able to collect all that they owed per year. Since don Pedro took pride in not having fallen behind, he must have been paying the difference himself. He could do this, thanks to his thriving muleteer business.

The tribute lists for the present year, 1658, here in San Pablo Tepemaxalco

† [Teocaltitlan] Tlatocapan †

v Don Gabriel de San Pedro ----------------------- 6 tt° [tostones]
v Francisco Nicolás ------------------------------- 6 tt°
v Bernabé de Santiago ----------------------------- 3 tt°
v Baltasar Gregorio ------------------------------- 6 tt°
v Juan Nicolás ------------------------------------ 6 tt°
v Francisco Nicolás ------------------------------- 6 tt°
v Juan Miguel------------------------------------- 6 tt°
v Francisca Juana --------------------------------- 3 tt°
v Don Diego de la Cruz---------------------------- 6 tt°
v Gabriel de Tapia ------------------------------- 6 tt°

v Juan Baptista------------------------------------- 6 tt°
v Micaela Elena, widow---------------------------- 3 tt°

† Pasiontitlan †

v Diego Jacobo------------------------------------- 6 tt°
v Nicolás Gaspar ---------------------------------- 6 tt°
v Melchior Francisco------------------------------- 6 tt°
v Lucas Lorenzo ----------------------------------- 6 tt°
v Gabriel de San Pedro ---------------------------- 6 tt°
v Diego Bernardo---------------------------------- 6 tt°
v Diego Hernández -------------------------------- 6 tt°
v Francisco Jaime --------------------------------- 6 tt°
v Juan Pablo -------------------------------------- 6 tt°
v Baltasar Reyes ---------------------------------- 6 tt°
v Francisco Martín--------------------------------- 6 tt°
v Juan Pascual ------------------------------------ 6 tt°
v Lorenzo Ignacio--------------------------------- 6 tt°
v Don Pedro Jacobo------------------------------- 6 tt°
v Gaspar Melchior--------------------------------- 3 tt°
v Juan Felipe ------------------------------------- 6 tt°
v Melchior Leonardo ------------------------------ 6 tt°
v Gabriel de Santiago------------------------------ 6 tt°
v Pedro de San Juan ------------------------------ 6 tt°
v Juan de Santiago-------------------------------- 6 tt°
v Diego Jacobo------------------------------------ 3 tt°
v Diego de la Cruz -------------------------------- 3 tt°
v Pedro de Santiago------------------------------- 3 tt°
v Pedro de San Juan ------------------------------ 3 tt°
v Don Pedro de la Cruz --------------------------- 6 tt°

† Tlatocapan †

v Estevan Nicolás --------------------------------- 6 tt°
v Francisco Martín--------------------------------- 6 tt°
v Sebastián de San Juan --------------------------- 6 tt°
v Clara Leonor, widow----------------------------- 3 tt°
v Juana Cristina, widow --------------------------- 3 tt°
v Juan Baptista------------------------------------ 6 tt°
v Pedro de la Cruz -------------------------------- 3 tt°
v Juana Andresa, widow --------------------------- 6 tt°

v Mateo Nicolás ------------------------------------ 6 ttº
v Clara Beatriz ------------------------------------- 6 ttº
v Isabel María, widow ----------------------------- 6 ttº
v Melchior de San Juan --------------------------- 6 ttº
v Francisco Hernández --------------------------- 6 ttº
v Martín Nicolás----------------------------------- 6 ttº
v Andrés de San Miguel --------------------------- 6 ttº
v Pedro Juantzin ---------------------------------- 6 ttº
v Diego Jacobo------------------------------------- 6 ttº
v Bernardino de Santiago-------------------------- 6 ttº
v Antona Clara ------------------------------------ 3 ttº
v Baltasar de San Juan --------------------------- 6 ttº
v Sebastián Jacobo -------------------------------- 6 ttº
v Pablo de San Juan------------------------------- 6 ttº
v Juan Baptista------------------------------------ 6 ttº
v Juan Mateo -------------------------------------- 6 ttº

† Pochtlan †

v Nicolás Pedro ----------------------------------- 6 ttº
v Lucas Marcos ----------------------------------- 6 ttº
v Ambrosio de San Juan -------------------------- 6 ttº
v Don Mateo de San Francisco -------------------- 6 ttº
v Gabriel de San Francisco------------------------ 6 ttº
v Francisco Hernández --------------------------- 6 ttº
v Martín Gerónimo-------------------------------- 6 ttº
v Andrés de San Juan ----------------------------- 6 ttº
v Pedro de la Cruz -------------------------------- 6 ttº
v Juan Baptista------------------------------------ 6 ttº
v Andrés Hernández------------------------------- 6 ttº
v Juan Lucas -------------------------------------- 6 ttº
v Agustín Diego ----------------------------------- 6 ttº
v Petronila Lucía---------------------------------- 6 ttº
v Lucas de Santiago------------------------------- 6 ttº
v Juan Martín ------------------------------------- 6 ttº
v Paola Clara, widow ----------------------------- 3 ttº
v Lucas Martín------------------------------------ 3 ttº
v Melchior Cristóbal------------------------------ 6 ttº
v Andrés García ----------------------------------- 3 ttº

† Mexicapan †

v Luis Damián ------------------------------------ 6 tt°
v Francisco Martín ---------------------------------- 6 tt°
v Juan Lucas -------------------------------------- 6 tt°
v Juan Rafael-------------------------------------- 6 tt°
v Juana Hernández, widow ------------------------- 3 tt°
v Matías Nicolás ----------------------------------- 6 tt°
v Andrés Nicolás ---------------------------------- 6 tt°
v Francisco Hernández ----------------------------- 6 tt°
v Francisca Agustina------------------------------- 6 tt°

Here will be entered the bachelors who will pay tribute in the year 1658:

v Andrés de Santiago ------------------------------ 3 tt°
v Agustín Salvador -------------------------------- 3 tt°
v Luzo López -------------------------------------- 3 tt°
v Pedro de la Cruz -------------------------------- 3 tt°
v Juan Diego -------------------------------------- 3 tt°
v Andrés de San Juan ------------------------------ 3 tt°
v Diego Jacobo------------------------------------- 3 tt°
v Bernabé de la Cruz ------------------------------ 3 tt°
v Pedro Nicolás ----------------------------------- 3 tt°
v Domingo Mendoza -------------------------------- 3 tt°
v Pedro Hernández -------------------------------- 3 tt°

† San Lucas Tlacatlan †

v Gabriel de Santiago------------------------------ 6 tt°
v Don Andrés de Santa María ---------------------- 6 tt°
v Juan de la Cruz --------------------------------- 6 tt°
v Felipe de la Cruz -------------------------------- 3 tt°
v Lucas Damián ----------------------------------- 6 tt°
v Lorenzo Rafael---------------------------------- 6 tt°
v Diego Nicolás----------------------------------- 6 tt°
v Miguel Melchior --------------------------------- 6 tt°
v Matías de San Miguel ---------------------------- 6 tt°
v Ventura de San Juan ----------------------------- 6 tt°
v Juan de la Torres -------------------------------- 6 tt°
v Juan Martín------------------------------------- 6 tt°
v Matías de San Francisco -------------------------- 6 tt°
v Martín de Santiago ------------------------------ 6 tt°

v Juan Melchior------------------------------------ 6 tt°
v Pablo de San Juan-------------------------------- 6 tt°
v Pedro Elías ------------------------------------- 6 tt°
v Lucas Damián ----------------------------------- 6 tt°
v Francisco de San Juan---------------------------- 6 tt°
v Cristóbal de San Juan---------------------------- 6 tt°
v Pedro Hernández -------------------------------- 6 tt°
v Miguel Cristóbal--------------------------------- 6 tt°
v Felipe Jacobo----------------------------------- 6 tt°
v Juan Matías ------------------------------------- 6 tt°
v Francisco Hernández ---------------------------- 6 tt°
v Pablo de San Juan-------------------------------- 6 tt°
v Miguel Matías ----------------------------------- 6 tt°
v Bernabé de San Juan----------------------------- 6 tt°

† Santa María [de la Asunción] †

v Nicolás Pedro ----------------------------------- 6 tt°
v Miguel Serrano ---------------------------------- 6 tt°
v Baltasar Andrés---------------------------------- 6 tt°
v Cristóbal Gabriel -------------------------------- 3 tt°
v Antón Juárez------------------------------------ 6 tt°
v Miguel Matías ----------------------------------- 6 tt°
v Diego de San Juan ------------------------------- 6 tt°
v Andrés García ----------------------------------- 6 tt°
v Mateo Juárez------------------------------------ 6 tt°
v Juan Baptista------------------------------------ 6 tt°
v Juan Alonso------------------------------------- 6 tt°
v Felipe de la Cruz -------------------------------- 6 tt°
v Joseph Hernández ------------------------------- 6 tt°
v Juan Pascual ------------------------------------ 6 tt°
v Joseph de la Cruz -------------------------------- 3 tt°
v Miguel Matías ----------------------------------- 6 tt°
v Diego Miguel ----------------------------------- 6 tt°
v Bernabé Antón---------------------------------- 6 tt°

† Santiago People †

v Juan de Santiago -------------------------------- 6 tt°
v Sebastián Serrano ------------------------------- 6 tt°
v Juan Pascual ------------------------------------ 6 tt°

v Mateo Serrano ----------------------------------- 6 tt°
v Joseph Francisco -------------------------------- 6 tt°
v ~~Pedro de San Gabriel~~6

Memorial of the tribute for the year 1658, Tepemaxalco, San Pablo

Teopancaltitlan [Tlatocapan]

◎◎◎◎◎◎◎◎◎◎◎◎ OOO
Today, Thursday, the 18th of July, Gabriel de Tapia came to count out
the tribute of twelve pesos and three tomines.   12 ps, 3 ts
◎◎◎◎◎◎◎◎ OO ◎◎
Today, in the year 1658, Gabriel de Tapia came to count out the
tribute of eight pesos and two tomines.

8 ps, 2 ts

Together they put in a request.[1]
Gabriel de Tapia was paid two pesos.   2 ps

On behalf of **Pasiontitlan**, the tribute for the year 1658:
◎◎◎◎◎◎◎◎◎◎◎◎◎◎◎◎◎ OOOOO
Today, Thursday, the 18th of July, Gabriel de San Pedro came to
count out the tribute of seventeen pesos and five tomines.   17 ps, 5 ts
Toston
◎ ◎◎◎◎◎◎◎◎◎◎
◎◎ OOO
Gabriel Pedro paid the tribute of ten pesos and [also a?] toston-peso.

11 ps

They put in a request.
◎◎◎
Gabriel Pedro was paid three pesos.   3 ps

On behalf of **Tlatocapan**, the tribute for the year 1658:
◎◎◎◎◎◎◎◎◎◎
◎◎◎◎◎◎◎ OOOOOO

---

1. The writer uses a Spanish loanword here (*suplican*). Within the next few
years, the notebook reveals that the practice of requesting that some of the tribute be
immediately returned to the subaltepetl's officers was discontinued. This was probably
because the subaltepetls were perennially in arrears. For a similar practice, albeit without use of a loanword, see Brylak, "Commissioning of an Image," in Olko, Sullivan,
and Szeminski, *Dialogue with Europe*, 283–86.

Today, Thursday, the 18th of July, Mateo Nicolás came to count out
the tribute, eighteen pesos and six tomines.   18 ps, 6 ts
They put in a request.
Three pesos, three tomines were counted out. It was all paid to
Mateo Nicolás.
◎◎◎ ○○○

On behalf of **Pochtlan**, the tribute for the year 1658:
◎◎◎◎◎◎◎◎◎◎
◎◎◎◎◎◎◎◎◎◎
◎◎
Today, Saturday, the 20th of July, Lucas de Santiago came to count
out the tribute of twenty-four pesos.

                                                               24 ps

Toston
◎ ◎◎◎◎◎◎◎◎◎◎◎◎◎◎
Today, in the year 1658, Lucas de Santiago came to count out the
tribute of fifteen pesos and four tomines.   15 ps, 4 ts

The tribute pertaining to **San Lucas** in the year 1658:
◎◎◎◎◎◎◎◎◎
◎◎◎◎◎◎◎◎◎
◎◎◎◎◎◎ ○○○
Today, Thursday, the 18th of July, the San Lucas tribute was counted
out, twenty-six pesos and three tomines. Don Pablo de San Juan,
past alcalde; Gabriel de Santiago, juez; Matías Francisco, tribute
collector.   26 ps, 3 ts
They put in a request. Past alcalde don Pablo de San Juan was paid
four pesos, three-and-a-half tomines.   4 ps, 3 ts, half
◎◎◎◎ ○○○ ☉

The tribute pertaining to **Santa María de la Asunción** in the year
1658:[2]
◎◎◎◎◎◎◎◎◎◎◎◎◎◎◎◎◎◎◎◎◎

---

2. This is the last listing for the year. Neither Mexicapan nor Santiago are
recorded as bringing tribute payments in this or any other year. The tribute rolls
indicate that they were very small communities. Probably they did not elect their own
officers but rather gave their payments to another subaltepetl's officers.

◎◎◎ OOO OOO
Today, Sunday, the 2nd of February, Juan Baptista, past councilman, paid tribute of twenty pesos.
◎◎◎◎◎◎◎◎◎
◎◎◎◎ OOOO Toston
Today, Sunday, the 2nd of February, Juan Baptista, past councilman of Santa María, paid tribute of ten pesos.[3]

3. The numbers written out are lower than the numbers pictorially represented, yet there is no record of a request having been put in for some of the money to be returned. Was that accidentally omitted? Or did the subaltepetl owe some sort of fine for paying not in July 1658 but rather February 1659? We cannot know.

Document 3: Parish Records of the Birth of Don Juan de la Cruz's
Siblings (1640s)

*In the early seventeenth century, in a large, leather-bound volume at the
convento of the Franciscan order in Calimaya, the indigenous people of
the region made written entries about each of the babies they baptized
at their beautiful, hand-painted fountain (see page xii). They organized
their record by tlaxilacalli and wrote their notations in Nahuatl. Then the
friar, also an ordained priest, who had done the baptism would sign his
name. (In addition, a higher level clergyman would periodically inspect
the book and sign it, indicating that it passed muster.) These methods
probably dated from the postconquest days, when the indigenous people
simply had to do all church business on their own, as a visiting friar or
priest was all their town could ever expect to see. However, in the Toluca
region, as all across Mexico, parish records were increasingly kept in
Spanish, by Spaniards, and according to European norms. In the parish
records of Calimaya, the old volume reveals just that process: we see the
entries being taken over by Spanish friars themselves as they recorded the
names of the children they baptized.*

*More can be gleaned from these old records than the gradual process
of Hispanicization that was occurring. One might, for example, study
the patterns of who was chosen to be the godparent of whose child
and then think about why. One can also catch glimpses of what were
sometimes painful family dramas. For instance, there was a time
lapse between the birth of don Juan de la Cruz and a string of younger
siblings. In that interval we see an entry that appears to mark the birth
of a son to don Juan's father, but by a woman who was not his mother.
Likewise, we see the birth of a boy named Felipe whose parentage in*

that small town was supposedly unknown, but who was brought to the church by "Pedro +" (almost certainly indicating Pedro de la Cruz); we also know that Pedro raised a son named Felipe who received nothing in his will (see the introduction). Alone these parish records tell us little more than who was born, but, in the context of other records, they are illuminating.

These records are preserved in the Archivo Parroquial de San Pedro y San Pablo in Calimaya, Mexico.

[In Nahuatl]
Pasiontitlan. Francisca. July 20, 1641. Her honored father was Nicolás Gaspar,[1] her honored mother, Leonor Luisa. And the godfather: Lorenzo López.

    [signed in a different handwriting] Fray Francisco de Luis

Pasiontitlan. Today, Wednesday, the 20-2 [sic][2] of November 1645, was baptized a child named Francisca. Her honored father was Nicolás Gaspar, her honored mother, María de la Cruz. Her godfather was Juan Pablo, her godmother, Angelina Francisca.

    [signed in a different handwriting] Fray Baltasar de Echaburra

[Later in the volume, now in Spanish]
Isabela
On the 2nd of September 1647, I baptized Isabel, the daughter of Nicolás Gaspar and of María de la Cruz. The godmother was Angelina Francisca.

                  Fray Juan de Guernica

Phelipe[3]
On the 2nd of February 1649, I baptized Phelipe, a child of unknown parents. The godparents were Juan Phelipe and Pedro +

                  Fray Juan de Guernica

1. This is likely to have been don Juan's father having a child out of wedlock, as there were no other men by that name in Pasiontitlan. However, it is conceivable that a local woman who lived in Pasiontitlan had a child by an outsider who also happened to be named Nicolás Gaspar.
2. In Nahuatl the number twenty would be expressed as "two tens and two," hence the apparently odd formation.
3. This is likely a record of the birth of don Juan's future (illegitimate) brother-in-law, Felipe de la Cruz.

Nicolás[4]
The 8th of September of the present year of 1649, I baptized Nicolás, son of Nicolás Gaspar and of María de la Cruz. The godparents were Juan de la Cruz and Francisca Angelina, his wife.[5]

I sign: Fray Antonio Tovar y Ulloa

Diego
On the 29th of July 1652, I baptized Diego, son of Nicolás Gaspar and of María de la Cruz. The godparents were Pascual López and Juan Ortiz.[6]

Fray Juan de Guernica

4. This child must have died young, for when don Juan as an old man happily remembered the names of all his younger brothers and sisters he did not include Nicolás. He did include one named Juana, who for some reason does not appear in the baptismal volume. Perhaps she was baptized elsewhere, or perhaps she never received the sacrament.

5. This was probably don Pedro's father and his then wife, as we know the families were close.

6. Juan Ortiz was probably Spanish, as the name does not appear in the tribute notebook for Tepemaxalco.

Document 4: The Will of Don Pedro de la Cruz (1667)

Wills have long been used by social historians to explore the material elements of real people's lives. How much land did they have, and where did they get it? How many children did they have, and how did they divide property between them? What sorts of material goods did they have in their houses? Was it common to borrow or lend money? And so on. But wills can also reveal cultural aspects of people's lives, and they can help us to trace connections between people who would otherwise appear as isolated names in the archive.

Spaniards taught the Nahuas to dictate their wills in their own language, and the people responded with alacrity, probably because the custom was reminiscent of the kind of perorations dying relatives had often made in the years before the conquest. It became normal practice to send for a notary when one was near death; there is often a highly performative element in these testaments, which were issued at a dramatic moment in the family's history. All across central Mexico, many Nahuatl wills remained in local church archives. Some, however, made their way to Mexico City for storage; these tended to be paired with official Spanish translations produced by employees of the Crown's government—and so it was with the wills of the wealthy De la Cruz family. In fact, in the case of don Pedro's will, the original Nahuatl document has been lost, and only the Spanish translation survives.

In 1667 don Pedro must have thought he was dying. As we know from his family record book, he recovered. We thus have a snapshot of his life at an earlier moment than death, when his daughter was married and had three young children, but her youngest children were not yet born. Someone named Felipe de la Cruz is credited with having written out the will; we know from the De la Cruz family record group that he was a son of don Pedro, but here we learn that he was to receive no inheritance. He may have been illegitimate. (There is further evidence for that in the parish records, as we have seen.) What else can be learned about don Pedro and his life when this document is read carefully? We might, for instance, make an argument that we see a deep trust in his son-in-law, a fondness for his firstborn grandchild, Jacinto, and a belief that his wife will be able to carry on without him.

This will is preserved in Mexico City, Archivo General de la Nación, Tierras 1501, expediente 3, folios 13–14v.

[fol. 13]
Jesus, Mary, and Joseph =

May the names of God the father, God Christ, and God the Holy Spirit be always praised. May it be done this way, Amen. Jesus, Mary, and Joseph.

Now, Wednesday, the 18th of March of the year of 1667, I place my last will and testament; my name is don Pedro de la Cruz, gobernador = in the town of San Pedro and San Pablo Tepemaxalco; my home is in the street they call Pasiontitlan. Since my body and flesh is ill, and if God would want to take my life and I die, in his hands I recommend my soul, and in the hands of the most holy Virgen Mary and of Lord San Miguel Arcangel and of San Juan Bautista and of Lord San Joseph and of the patron saints San Pedro and San Pablo, and in those of all the male and female saints that are in heaven, may all speak for me to God, our lord; may it be done this way. Amen, Jesus.

1 First, I notify that, if God takes away my life, my grave will be opened in the church where my dear father is buried; there my body will be buried.

2 Second, I notify that, if God takes away my life, my body will be wrapped in the habit of our father San Francisco.

3 Third, I notify that twelve masses and twelve responsory prayers will be said for my soul, and that my loved father will bury me with a High Mass with vigil and responsory prayers, and for it he will get sixty-two pesos.

4 Fourth, I notify that one arroba of wax will be bought, and 23 pesos will be given for it. Also, I notify that one arroba and a half of meat, and one fanega of corn will be distributed to the poor.

5 Fifth, I notify that I contribute 3 pesos to [the fund for] Holy Jerusalem.

6 Sixth, I order and notify that the cantores will get 3 pesos.

7 Seventh, I notify that the Souls will be given 3 pesos.

Also, I notify that I leave 1 peso and 4 reales to the cofradía of my Señora de la Concepción == 8 Eighth, I notify that to the most holy Virgin of Guadalupe,

[verso]

for whom I made a chapel, and I put her in it, I give a field in Pelaxtitlan, and a corncrib, and the corn in it, and oxen, and sheep; they are of my Lady of Guadalupe, and the other half I leave for Jesús Nazareno, and all the land that is in the field, so that my grandchildren would plow it; it is my will, and I say that myself and my son-in-law don Juan de la Cruz, we opened [started to cultivate] it, so that no one is ever to say a word.

9 And as well I notify that to my wife, whose name is doña Ana Juana, I leave some money and corn to raise my grandchildren, and all the field that is in Otlaltenco, Santa María en el Camino, I leave it to her and to my son-in-law don Juan de la Cruz, the two of us opened that land, and of my will I leave it to them; no one is to say anything.

10 As well I notify that I have a grandchild named Jacinto, I leave him 30 mules, 20 of them in pairs and 10 in [Pelaxtitlan?]; no one is ever to say a word to him.

11 As well I notify that I leave, and it is my will, to my wife, doña Ana Juana, a piece of land in Atlaltenco; no one is ever to say a word to her.

12 Also, I notify that to one daughter named Josepha Francisca I leave money, land, and corn.

13 Also I notify that the whole field in Santa María en el Camino de la Asunción that goes through Tenango, I leave it to my grandchildren, Jacinto and the other one named Josepha; no one is ever to say anything.

14 As well I notify that this big house with the saints and all that is in there, I leave it to Jacinto so that he will take care of it.

15 Also I notify that to my other grandchild called Pedro I leave the house on the other side, and all the field land in Quiquichtepeque; no one is ever to say anything.

[fol. 14]
As well I notify that I leave to the same grandchild of mine Pedro [?] mares and 8 mules; no one is ever to take them from him.
As well I notify that I leave to my grandchild called Josepha the entire house in front of the church; no one is ever to take it from her.
And as well I notify that I have a house in Calimaya, which belonged to don Matías de San Francisco, gobernador; it is mine and I bought it; no one is ever to say anything.
And as well I notify in front of God that I do not have any leftover debt in this town, and what is due to me needs to be paid by those who owe me from the mules and the steers they deduct, 120 pesos to be collected.
And here I finish my will and testament, I, don Pedro de la Cruz, gobernador, before my witnesses; it is my will, and I notify that my executors are my wife, doña Ana Juana, and my son-in-law don Juan de la Cruz. I notify that they are my executors, and I pray Lord Captain [or capellán?] Francisco Arias to help my executors; I did not call him since he is not here, but with all my will I appoint him as support to my executors in case they ever have a problem. And I pray that my notary put my signature
Don Pedro de la Cruz, gobernador, I signed when the testament was done =
Don Francisco Jiménez, alcalde = Don Nicolás Gaspar, alcalde
Juan Bautista, *juez mayor* = Don Antonio Valeriano, past alcalde =
Don Nicolás Blas, alcalde of Santa María de la Asunción = Don Juan Martín, alcalde of San Lucas =
Don Juan Pedro, past alcalde; Don Juan Diego, fiscal of the holy church =
Agustín Salvador, notary of the holy church =

I wrote it, Felipe de la Cruz, notary of the commonwealth =

The will of don Juan de la Cruz is one of the longest and most impressive of the surviving Nahuatl testaments of the Toluca Valley in the colonial era. Unlike don Pedro's will, which was the product of a sudden illness or injury, don Juan's was obviously written over time with great care and thought. He reports that he is sick—and epidemic disease was indeed rife in 1691—but the document is clearly not the work of a few moments. He recounts all the family history he believes is necessary regarding the main distribution of the property, and he includes numerous small bequests. By now, in the 1690s, the De la Cruz family fortune is significant indeed. Each of don Juan's children by his first wife—through whom he gained access to the fortune—inherits a house and land. Even his four littlest children, by his second wife, receive something substantial: the right to go on living in their present home, as well as a piece of land and a horse and some oxen for each. This was not at all typical among Mexico's rural indigenous people. It is little wonder that the family considered that they had a special role to play in the commonwealth and that they thus worked hard to leave records behind, both written documents and artwork in the town's churches. As historians, we must be grateful that they felt this way! Don Juan's will was a crucial building block in the project of tracing the De la Cruz family history.

The document reveals fascinating cultural nuance as well. Three different times don Juan mentions that he is leaving a single child a house and the responsibility of caring for a statue of a saint. Then he orders that no one is ever to try to take the property from "them." He—and undoubtedly the children as well—seems to think of the saint as if *it were another person. This will is preserved in Mexico City, Archivo General de la Nación, Tierras 2533, expediente 5, folios 1–2v.*

[fol. 1]

Jesus, Mary, and Joseph

v May the precious revered name of God, the father; [God, his son]; and God, the Holy Spirit, three persons but really only a single, really true deity, God, the Holy Trinity, be entirely praised. May it be done, Amen. Jesus, Mary, and Joseph, etc.

v Today, Saturday, the 18th of August of the year of 1691, I, don Juan de la Cruz, am lying sick of the illness that our lord God has sent upon me; I do not know what will happen to me. I say that I am a Christian, and I believe in the Holy Trinity, the three divine persons, God, the father; God, his son; and God the Holy Spirit, but really just one true divinity God, and I believe all that our mother, the holy church, deems true.

v First I say that my father, Nicolás Gaspar, and my mother, María de la Cruz, have died; they raised me and arranged my marriage before dying, and they left me two rows of magueyes. And I say that I have brothers and sisters; the eldest is my brother Melchior Francisco, [then] Francisca Angelina, Isabel Martina and Juana and Diego de Santiago. My precious father left all of their inheritance divided among them. I say that I married with my wife doña Josepha Francisca; my father-in-law was don Pedro de la Cruz and my mother-in-law doña Ana Juana, and the land and houses that my late father-in-law and mother-in-law left were the big house, with a San Pedro, and a large corncrib and a large piece of land at Santa María next to the *calvario.* She [my wife doña Josepha Francisca] took half, and her sister Josepha de la Cruz took the other half. And I gave [the sister and her husband] two yokes of oxen, a horse with saddle, and three rows of magueyes. I, don Juan de la Cruz, and I, doña Josepha Francisca, arranged their marriage. My children are not ever to show envy [try to get her share], [particularly?] my eldest Jacinto de la Cruz.

v And I gave to Josepha de la Cruz, my daughter, a house and San Pedro and San Diego and half of a cultivated field that she shares with Jacinto de la Cruz and a corncrib, two yokes of oxen, a horse with saddle, and three rows of magueyes. No one is ever to say anything. We arranged the marriage of this daughter of ours. No one is ever to show envy.

y̱ And to another daughter of mine, named Juana de la Cruz, I gave a house, and I am giving her San Juan and a piece of land at the edge of the tribute field, two yokes of oxen, a horse with saddle, a corncrib, and three rows of magueyes. And we arranged her marriage. No one is ever to say anything.

y̱ And to a son of mine, Pedro de la Cruz, I gave a house, and I gave him a Jesús Nazareno and a Jesús Niño—he is to serve them—and a piece of land,

[fol. 1v]

a corncrib, two yokes of oxen, a horse with saddle, and three rows of magueyes. We likewise arranged the marriage of our children [Pedro and his wife]. No one is to say anything.

y̱ And I by myself arranged the marriage of another daughter of mine named María de la Cruz; my late wife had already died. I am giving her a corncrib and three rows of magueyes, and I give her our precious revered mother of Nativitas, a horse with saddle, two yokes of oxen, and a piece of land on the road to Tenanco.

y̱ And I order that to my son Agustín de la Cruz, unmarried, I give a statue of San Josef—he is to serve it—a corncrib and two yokes of oxen, a horse with saddle, and a cultivated field on the road to Santa María. He is not to leave, for I am leaving him inside this house. And I am giving him three rows of magueyes. No one is ever to say anything to them.[1]

y̱ And I order that to another son of mine, named Bernabé de la Cruz, I leave my precious revered father San Antonio—he is to serve him—a corncrib, three rows of magueyes, a piece of land in Coyohuacan, next to a tejocote tree [or in Texocotitlan], two yokes of oxen and a horse, and he is to be given a saddle. He is not to leave; they are to be here inside this, my home. No one is to say anything to them.

y̱ And I order that to my little daughter named Nicolasa de la Cruz I leave a San Bernardo—she is to serve him—and she is to be given a corncrib, and she is to be given three rows of magueyes, and she

1. This is the first of several places where the grammar indicates that a saint is being considered as another person.

is to be given two yokes of oxen, and she is to be given a horse and a saddle. And she is not to leave; she is to be here and to serve the saints. No one is ever to say anything to them. And I am giving a piece of land at Tepetonco to Nicolasa de la Cruz.

v And I order that to another [child], my youngest, named Ignacio de la Cruz, I am giving a San Ignacio, as well as a Santa Gertrudis and a corncrib, and he is to be given three rows of magueyes, two yokes of oxen, a piece of land at the large body of water, a horse, and my saddle. That is what I am giving him; no one is ever to take it from him.

v And to my wife named doña Melchora María I order that they are to give a yoke of oxen, two rows of magueyes up above [meaning up the hill]—they are to go show them to her—and they are to give her 20 fanegas of shelled maize, and I order that no one is ever to say anything to her.

v And I order that my grave is to be opened facing my precious revered father, San Antonio [in the church]; the brothers [of the cofradía] are responsible for it, for I belong to the holy cofradía [of San Antonio], and I am giving five magueyes to San Antonio.

v And my shroud that I will wear is to be the habit of San Francisco, and I will be girt with San Francisco's rope.

[fol. 2]
And I order that three masses and three responsory prayers are to be said for me; they will be the help of my soul. And four pounds of candles are to be bought.

v And I order that I am giving 4 reales for Jerusalem.

v And to [the cofradía of] the holy sacrament I am giving a peso. And to the cantores I am giving a peso.

v And I order that to the orphan named Juana I am giving eight small magueyes; she is to tear them out [of the ground]; they are to be pointed out to her.

v And here in public I say that I spent four years as gobernador; I did well in completing the quota of tribute collected; I owe nothing. No one is ever to say anything to my children, for all the books are there in which are designated what was spent as expenses. The citizens [or authorities] of the altepetl are never to say that I owe them anything.

<u>v</u> And I bought *chirimías* [musical instruments]. I am giving them to my children [in a figurative sense] the cantores; with them they are to serve my precious revered mother Guadalupe.

It was all still there on a brisk October morning in 2017. As we stood on top of a pedestrian bridge at the town's entrance, the De la Cruz family world was still visible to us—the bell tower of the main church of Calimaya at the center and, just a few blocks north, the tower of the church in Santa María de la Asunción. On the horizon the peaks of the Nevado de Toluca and the hill of Tepemaxalco were watching over our wanderings, as they had over the lives of don Pedro, don Juan, and their wives and children almost four hundred years before.[1]

We were struck on our visit by the enduring sense of local belonging and pride, together with the buildings, the roads, and the landscape. The people in each neighborhood still treasured their churches, festivals, and history, with roots deep in the past and yet at the same time very present: small, ancient stones carved in the shape of an indigenous face still looked out from the walls of the church and the open chapel. People still shared responsibilities for music, decorations, and food provided for celebrations all year round, as well as a sense of duty to their community. It was as if the spirit of don Pedro, and many a governor and mayordomo, lived on.

At the heart of the festivals and church buildings, today like centuries ago, are very special members of the community: the saints. For everybody, San Pedro and San Pablo (in their separate niches after the *pleito de los santos*), San Francisco, and the Virgen de los Angeles (once Santa María de la Asunción) are tangible entities to whom people offer not only candles and prayers but food and music, perhaps even a piece of land. At the same time, the saints are much

---

1. Nowadays the town of Calimaya has taken over the whole area, and Tepemaxalco no longer exists per se.

more than material, acting as mediators and gatekeepers to the sacred.

For us, walking the streets of Calimaya-Tepemaxalco, visiting its churches, and meeting its inhabitants made visible the relevance of colonial documents such as the De la Cruz family papers. The sense of community, the sharing of duties, and the myriad forms of local religion all have a long history, built day in and day out by people like don Pedro and don Juan. They spent their energies and skills on behalf of their altepetl, helping preserve traditions and buildings that remain at the core of the identity of the place still today. Yet their actions also reflected the interests of their family as well as conscious, individual choices. The documents they produced and passed down to their descendants allow for a view as rare as it is significant into the personal aspirations and inclinations of indigenous individuals, beyond the communal dimension. The indigenous people of Mexico had most certainly experienced conquest, but their writings in the ensuing generations show that, in important regards, they had not been vanquished: they still knew who they were, both as individuals and as a community, and they made sure that posterity would not entirely forget either.

The written form of Nahuatl in the Toluca Valley displays some shifts due in part to transformations across time that were widespread throughout Mexico but also to some local traits that distinguish this variant of Nahuatl from others. The language of the De la Cruz papers is no exception, and, while the topic of Toluca Valley Nahuatl has been covered in detail elsewhere, here we present some general aspects.[1]

Given the period in which the various hands composed the papers, the text shows the shift from stage 2 to stage 3 Nahuatl, as explained by James Lockhart.[2] In the text it is common to see the weakening of syllable-final consonants, as well as the frequent omission of syllables, typical of stage 3 everywhere but even more so for Toluca Valley Nahuatl. To give just some examples: the *w* sound disappears so that we find *tlapalique* for *tlapaliuque* (working men), and *l* disappears in *sepohuali* for *cempohualli* (twenty).

Something similar happens with syllable-final *n*, often omitted in standard Nahuatl and particularly in this area. Thus we see *ichatzinco* for *ichantzinco* (the home of) and *totlaçonatzin* for

1. See Lockhart, "Toward Assessing the Phoneticity," and Pizzigoni, *Testaments of Toluca*, 33–40.

2. The stages of development of the Nahuatl language were first proposed in Karttunen and Lockhart, *Nahuatl in the Middle Years*, and later fully explained in the conclusion of Lockhart, *Nahuas After the Conquest*, as well as expanded to deal with language and culture. Stage 1 covers the first postconquest generation (to about 1540 or 1545), and during this period both language and culture changed very little. In stage 2, from 1550 to 1650, a myriad of words from Spanish, mainly nouns, entered the Nahuatl language, and change predominantly affected corporations. Finally, during stage 3, from 1650 on, Nahuatl took words other than nouns, created equivalences between Nahuatl and Spanish words, and added Spanish sounds to its phonology, while on the cultural side there were more intimate, structure-altering changes at the corporate as well as at the household level.

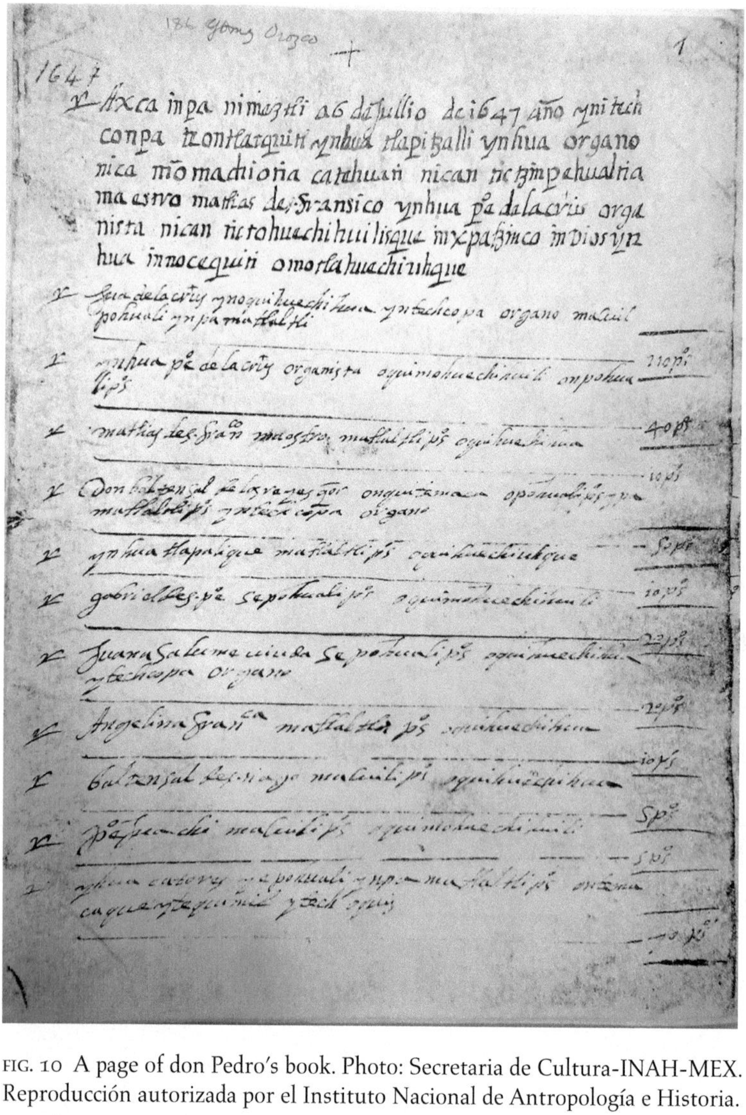

FIG. 10 A page of don Pedro's book. Photo: Secretaria de Cultura-INAH-MEX. Reproducción autorizada por el Instituto Nacional de Antropología e Historia.

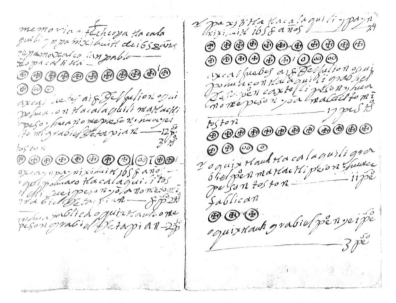

FIG. 11 A page of the tribute notebook. Photo: Secretaria de Cultura-INAH-MEX. Reproducción autorizada por el Instituto Nacional de Antropología e Historia.

totlaçonantzin (our precious mother). The consonant *n* is also added after a vowel to preserve it, such as in *ynhua* for *yhuan* (and), *itech-conpa* for *itechcopa* (concerning), and *yntoca/yntonca* for *ytoca* (his/her name). This is again common practice in stage 3 standard Nahuatl and was even more common in Toluca Valley Nahuatl, with examples such as *Tepemexalcon, Antonion,* and *concoliztli* for *cocoliztli* (epidemic). Another feature of stage 3 across central Mexico is vowel elision, especially between the possessive prefix and the possessed, but here our area is quite peculiar in the sense of *not* doing it to the normal extent. So instead of *naxca* for "my property" we find *noaxca* (*no-* possessive prefix).

However, for every example given here, we also find more standard spellings through the documents, and some of the very peculiar traits of Toluca Valley Nahuatl are actually not there or happen very late. For instance, the most common case of weakening of syllable-final consonants, final *tl,* here happens only much later: by the 1730s there is an instance of *xihuit* instead of *xihuitl* (year). And a most notable phenomenon, seen only in stage 3 Toluca Valley, the insertion

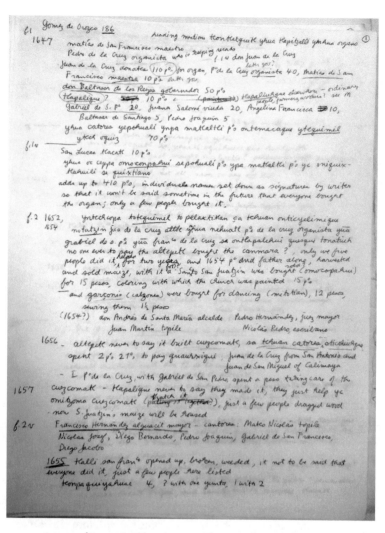

FIG. 12 A page of James Lockhart's notes. Photo: authors.

of an *i* after a vulnerable syllable-final consonant to preserve it in speech and writing (so that for *ixquich*, for example, we find *ixiquichi*, for "all") is not present at all. As a matter of fact, the entries for the first couple of decades display the regular spelling and phrases typical of stage 2 texts across central Mexico. Things become more irregular toward the end of the 1670s, when a new generation has taken over from don Pedro: the use of the extra *n* spreads (*conhualoni* for a "purchase," *chiconme* for "seven," *notlasontatzin* for "my precious father," *De lan Cruz* for "de la Cruz"), and more consonants are lost (*matlacpouali ypā naupouali* for *matlacpohualli ypan nauhpohualli*, for "two hundred" and "eighty"). It is this combination of stage 3 traits and Toluca Valley peculiarities with more standard spelling and absence of the extreme traits of Toluca Valley Nahuatl that makes us define the De la Cruz papers as in transition from stage 2 to stage 3.[3]

A last aspect of this transition is the use of loanwords from Spanish. The De la Cruz papers show the adoption of many Spanish nouns, as is to be expected, with some adaptation. Just to mention a few, we find *ce semana*, for "one week" (*ce* for "one" in Nahuatl), *cielo* for "sky," *comonidad* for "community," *libro* for "book," *jurametin* from *juramento* (translated in the text as "to swear"), and *destigos* for "witnesses" (*testigos*), as well as a host of Spanish terms referring to Spanish food and Christian offices and tools. With the passing of time we start finding turns of phrases or expressions, such as *porcecio tlalli* for "possession of the land" (from *posesión* in Spanish and *tlalli* in Nahuatl), *asta ynpa Lunes*, for "until Monday" (*hasta* and *lunes* in Spanish), and *ytiepo S^{or} don Simo Allde ma^o* for "in the time of señor don Simon being alcalde mayor" (using *tiempo* in Spanish). And, finally, Spanish verbs: in 1679 we find *omocobraro* (from *cobrar* in Spanish, "to charge") and *omoestrenado* (from *estrenar*, "to bring out") and, in the 1730s, *ocostaroc* (from *costar*, "to cost") and *quimontarua* (from *montar*, "to put together"). This phenomenon again confirms the transitional aspect of the documents.

Going beyond the peculiarities of Toluca Valley Nahuatl and the expected traits of stage 3, something else may be at play in the

---

3. A Nahuatl text cannot be placed securely in stage 3 just because it is written after 1650. In places such as the Toluca Valley, the transition between stage 2 and stage 3 may have taken longer. See Pizzigoni, *Life Within*.

documents. It seems that with the passing of time the knowledge of written Nahuatl simply declined over the generations, at least in this family. From the late 1640s to the 1670s, when don Pedro de la Cruz was governor, the entries show great command of the language and standard spellings for the most part. From 1678 on, when he was no longer governor and in charge of the account, we see a hyperuse of the extra *n*, at times going beyond what one could reasonably expect. And we also find examples that are closer to actual mistakes rather than language evolution, such as "Don Ju° de lla Cruz" with the weird *lla*, "Donn atoyo Ju°res" with the double *n*, two unusual spellings for Antonio (Anttonio and Antonion), and *rexidor manor* instead of the usual *regidor menor*, as well as something like *omoyetzticataca* for *omoyezticatca*, or "died." Vocabulary and expressiveness did not diminish, however, even if the education level did, and the language preserved the richness and color of times past, as the entries for the year 1677, for instance, illustrate.

To conclude, we offer a note on the orthography we used in the transcription. We decided to reproduce the punctuation any time it is present in the original text, and the same for some details such as the use of *i* versus *1* in numbers. On the other hand, we opted for less than extreme faithfulness in one particular regard: at odd times in the documents the word-final *l* looks like *r* or vice versa, and the two were probably pronounced the same way, at least by some people. We resolved the issue by using *l* in all those cases which use *l* today and *r* where that is the letter now expected (so we have *ytlaol* and *algua-cil* but *pintor* instead of *pintol*, to give some examples). Finally, we would point out that *pahui* (to add) is often used for *pohui*, "Jusepha" for "Josepha," and so forth, so one gets a sense of long, relaxed vowels being used in Tepemaxalco, but since the handwriting sometimes makes it unclear as to which is meant, we have regularized the spelling.

Most of these terms come from Spanish (S) or Nahuatl (N).

alcalde (S).   A leading member of the indigenous town council (cabildo). Sometimes referred to as an *alcalde ordinario*, probably to distinguish the position from an alcalde mayor. Toward the end of the eighteenth century, the alcaldes on the cabildo grew in number and were distinguished by rank so that we find a few references to an *alcalde menor*.

alcalde mayor (S).   Chief Spanish judicial and administrative official, governing over a large area including multiple altepetl.

altepetl (N).   Nahuatl word for any state, no matter how large, but mostly used to refer to a local ethnic state, like Tepemaxalco.

annals.   Term scholars have used to refer to the Nahuatl genre of the *xiuhpohualli*. The term was borrowed from Europe, where it has been used to refer to a medieval genre of history writing.

arroba (S).   Spanish unit of weight (about twenty-five pounds) or of volume (about four gallons).

barrio (S).   A neighborhood. It was often used in central Mexico as the equivalent of a tlaxilacalli.

bol (S).   Called "bole" in English, this compound is still used by artisan gilders. It is a very fine clay containing iron oxide as well as calcium and magnesium in varying proportions.

cabecera (S).   Head town. The Spaniards declared certain towns to be tax-collecting head towns, depending largely on preconquest political arrangements. This text inaccurately applies the term to the most powerful subaltepetl of Tepemaxalco.

cabildo (S).   A council, used to describe a session of any governing assembly, such as a municipal government or cathedral chapter, but most frequently to refer to the local indigenous council governing its internal affairs.

calvario (S).   Calvary, referring to constructions ranging from a wayside cross to a small chapel or sometimes even a collection of tiny chapels representing the stations of the cross.

camino (S).   Road.

cantor (pl. *cantores*) (S).   Singer, but borrowed into Nahuatl to refer to any kind of church musician.

chirimía (S).   Colonial wind instrument resembling an oboe.

cihuatepixqui (N).   Literally, "woman keeper or guardian of people." The word, found rarely in colonial documents, is always used in conjunction with a woman who had authority over other women in the community, often but not always in the context of a church organization, such as a cofradía.

cofradía (S).   Confraternity or sodality, a lay religious organization. Common people often joined a cofradía connected with their church, paying small dues in exchange for surety in times of crisis or the cost of a funeral.

Conde (S).   Count (title of nobility).

convento (S).   An institution housing either nuns or friars. *Monastery* can be used but usually isn't the perfect term in English, because the latter is understood to house monks who lived in isolation from the world. *Friary* would be more correct.

corregidor (S).   Chief Spanish judicial and administrative officer of a given district, at times used interchangeably with alcalde mayor.

cuartillo (S).   A coin worth one-quarter of a *peso*.

discalced friars.   Mendicant orders whose members go entirely barefoot or wear only sandals, symbolic of their vow of poverty.

don, doña (S).   High title attached to a first name, like "Sir" or "Lady" in English. It was applied by the Nahuas in this period only to titled nobility from Spain and to their own highest-status local indigenous nobility.

encomendero (S).   Recipient of an *encomienda*.

encomienda (S).   Grant, nearly always to a Spaniard, of the right to receive labor and tribute payments from a particular altepetl.

escribano (S).   Notary, clerk, scribe. This important position was attached to the indigenous cabildo.

fanega (S).   Unit of dry measurement, equivalent to about one-and-a-half bushels.

fiscal (S).   Chief steward of an indigenous church.

gobernador, gobernadora (S).   Governor, used by the Nahuas to refer to the highest office in the altepetl, the head of the cabildo.

guardián (S).   The friar at the head of a convento.

habit.   A long garment worn by a member of a religious order. The Nahuas often requested that their bodies be shrouded in a habit after their death.

hacendado (S).   The owner of a hacienda, or extensive landed property, usually a Spaniard.

juez (S).   Judge. Indigenous judges were appointed to act in their communities. Often it was the gobernador who also acted as judge. Only some community cases were taken up by the Spanish court system.

litter.   Platform used to carry religious icons in procession. It can also be used to carry coach-like seating for dignitaries to ride in.

macehualli (pl. *macehualtin*) (N).   Indigenous commoner.

maestro (S). A "master" in an artistic sense. A *maestro de capilla* was a choir master.

maguey (S, from Arawak). Agave plant. It was the source both of the alcoholic beverage *pulque* and of the fibers used to make paper and string.

maize (S, from Arawak). Corn.

Marquesado del Valle (S). Land grant given to Hernando Cortés and his heirs, encompassing a title of nobility (*marqués*) and *encomienda* rights to numerous altepetl.

Matlatzinca (N). The ethnic group living in the Toluca Valley before the conquest by the Mexica and their allies.

mayordomo (S). Steward, usually the main officer of a cofradía.

Mexica (N). The ethnic group that settled on an island in the middle of the central valley in the fourteenth century and later conquered extensive territories. Today they are most often (inaccurately) called the "Aztecs."

muleteer. Literally, a person who drives a mule train to transport goods. In colonial times the term was often used to describe a person who owned such a business.

Nahuas (N). Speakers of Nahuatl. At the time of the conquest, they inhabited most of central Mexico as well as more distant satellite communities.

Nahuatl (N). A language in the Uto-Aztecan family spoken by the Mexica and the people of dozens of other altepetl in Mexico. Due to the power of the Mexica, it became a lingua franca in the region.

pipiltin (N). Indigenous nobles.

principales (S). A Spanish term for indigenous nobles, often adopted by them.

real (pl. *reales*) (S). A silver coin worth one-eighth of a peso (hence "Spanish pieces of eight"), also the word for "royal."

rebeck. A two- or three-stringed instrument, played with a bow, common in medieval and Renaissance Europe.

regidor (S). A councilman, an elected member of the indigenous cabildo.

retablo (S). Altarpiece. In colonial Latin America these were often extraordinarily beautiful works of art.

secular clergy. Clergy (priests) who are not members of religious orders. In colonial Latin America friars had run most parishes before secular clergy began to arrive.

teopantlaca (N). Church people. In the sixteenth century the term referred to people with a church education or, sometimes, to those who held a church office.

tlapaliuque (N). Literally, "vigorous people." The term was used in the Toluca region to refer to adult men fit for work, commoners, those who were not *pipiltin*.

tlatoani (N). Literally, "he who speaks," a dynastic ruler of an altepetl, as in "chief" or "king." At first, the *tlatoani* took the role of *gobernador*, but gradually such dynastic lines died out, and soon any nobleman could be elected *gobernador*.

tlaxilacalli (N).   A constituent part of an altepetl.

tomín (pl. *tomines*) (S).   A coin worth one real. In Nahuatl sometimes it is used to refer to any coin.

tostón (pl. *tostones*) (S).   A coin worth half a peso. In Toluca it was the unit of measurement for the annual tribute payment.

tribute.   A payment made periodically by one state to another. After the demise of the *encomienda,* every indigenous altepetl owed tribute to the Spanish Crown. Each adult had to pay his or her equal share—in effect, a head tax.

villancico (S).   A genre of Spanish song popular in the Renaissance, poetry set to music, like a folk song.

xiuhpohualli (N).   Literally, "year count" or "yearly account," a preconquest oral genre used to recount history. After the conquest these performances were sometimes written down using the Roman alphabet; later such texts were called historical annals.

yoke.   A wooden contraption used to control a pair of oxen. In Nahuatl the term sometimes refers directly to a pair of oxen.

Anderson, Arthur J. O., and Susan Schroeder, eds. *Codex Chimalpahin*. Vol. 2. Norman: University of Oklahoma Press, 1997.

Borges, Pedro. *Religiosos en Hispanoamérica*. Madrid: MAPFRE.

Brylak, Agnieszka, ed. "Account of the Commissioning of an Image of the Virgin Mary, Tlaxcala, Mexico, 1600." In *Dialogue with Europe, Dialogue with the Past: Colonial Nahua and Quechua Elites in Their Own Words*, edited by Justyna Olko, John Sullivan, and Jan Szeminski, 283–86. Louisville: University Press of Colorado, 2018.

Christian, William, Jr. *Local Religion in Sixteenth-Century Spain*. Princeton: Princeton University Press, 1981.

Covarrubias Orozco, Sebastián de. *Tesoro de la lengua castellana, o española*. Madrid, 1611.

García Castro, René. *Indios, territorio, y poder en la provincia Matlatzinca: La negociación del espacio político de los pueblos otomianos, siglos XV–XVII*. Toluca: Colegio Mexiquense, 1999.

Gerhard, Peter. *A Guide to the Historical Geography of New Spain*. Cambridge: Cambridge University Press, 1972.

Gómez García, Lidia. *Los anales nahuas de la ciudad de Puebla de los Angeles, siglos XVI y XVIII*. Puebla: Ayuntamiento de Puebla, 2018.

Gruzinski, Serge. *La guerre des images: De Christophe Colomb à "Bladerunner."* Paris: Fayard, 1990.

Hernández Rodríguez, Rosaura. "La conquista española." In Rosenzweig et al., *Breve historia*, 65–76.

———. "Historia prehispanica." In Rosenzweig et al., *Breve historia*, 19–62.

Jarquín Ortega, María Teresa. "La formación de una nueva sociedad (siglos XVI y XVII)." In Rosenzweig et al., *Breve historia*, 77–139.

Karttunen, Frances, and James Lockhart. *Nahuatl in the Middle Years: Language Contact Phenomena in Texts of the Colonial Period*. Berkeley: University of California Press, 1976.

Lockhart, James. "Capital and Province, Spaniard and Indian: The Example of Late Sixteenth-Century Toluca." In *Provinces of Early Mexico: Variants of Spanish American Regional Evolution*, edited by Ida Altman and James Lockhart, 99–123. Los Angeles: UCLA Latin American Center, 1976.

———. *The Nahuas After the Conquest*. Stanford: Stanford University Press, 1992.

———. *Nahuas and Spaniards: Postconquest Central Mexican History and Philology*. Stanford: Stanford University Press, 1991.

———. "Spaniards Among Indians: Toluca in the Later Sixteenth Century." Chap. 12 in *Nahuas and Spaniards*, 202–41.

———. "Toward Assessing the Phoneticity of Older Nahuatl Texts: Analysis of a Document from the Valley of Toluca, Eighteenth Century." Chap. 8 in *Nahuas and Spaniards*, 122–40.

Loera y Chávez de Esteinou, Margarita. *Calimaya y Tepemaxalco: Tenencia y transmisión ereditaria de la tierra en dos comunidades indígenas; Epoca colonial*. Mexico City: Cuadernos de Trabajo del Departamento de Investigaciones Históricas, Instituto Nacional de Antropología e Historia, 1977.

———. *Memoria india en templos cristianos: Historia político-territorial y cosmovisión en San Antonio La Isla, San Lucas Tepemaxalco, y Amecameca; El Valle de Toluca y el Valle de México en el virreinato*. Mexico City: Instituto Nacional de Antropología e Historia, 2006.

Magazine, Roger. *The Village Is Like a Wheel: Rethinking Cargos, Family, and Ethnicity in Highland Mexico*. Tucson: University of Arizona Press, 2012.

Molina, Alonso. *Vocabulario en lengua castellana y mexicana*. 1571. Reprint, Mexico City: Porrúa, 1970.

Pizzigoni, Caterina. "In the Church and at Home: Approaches to Saints in Colonial Mexico." In *Formations of Belief: Historical Approaches to Religion and the Secular*, edited by Philip Nord, Katja Guenther, and Max Weiss, 106–25. Princeton: Princeton University Press, 2019.

———. *The Life Within: Local Indigenous Society in Mexico's Toluca Valley, 1650–1800*. Stanford: Stanford University Press, 2012.

———, ed. *Testaments of Toluca*. Stanford: Stanford University Press, 2007.

———. "Where Did All the Angels Go? An Interpretation of the Nahua Supernatural World." In *Angels, Demons, and the New World*, edited by Fernando Cervantes and Andrew Radden, 126–45. Cambridge: Cambridge University Press, 2013.

Ragon, Pierre. *Les saints et les images du Mexique (XVIᵉ–XVIIIᵉ siècle)*. Paris: L'Harmattan, 2003.

Rosenzweig, Fernando, Rosaura Hernández, María T. Jarquín, and Manuel Miño Grijalva, eds. *Breve historia del Estado de México*. Toluca: Colegio Mexiquense, 1987.

Townsend, Camilla. *Annals of Native America*. New York: Oxford University Press, 2016.

Wood, Stephanie. "Adopted Saints: Christian Images in Nahua Testaments of Late Colonial Toluca." *Americas* 47, no. 3 (1991): 259–93.

———. "Corporate Adjustments in Colonial Mexican Towns: Toluca Region, 1550–1810." PhD diss., University of California, Los Angeles, 1984.

Zapata y Mendoza, Juan Buenaventura. *Historia cronológica de la Noble Ciudad de Tlaxcala*. Edited and translated by Luis Reyes García and Andrea Martínez Baracs. Mexico City: Centro de Investigaciones y Estudios Superiores en Antropología Social, 1995.

Zárate Toscano, Verónica. *Los nobles antes la muerte en México: Actitudes, ceremonias, y memoria (1750–1850)*. Mexico City: Colegio de México and Instituto Mora, 2000.

latin american originals

Series Editor | Matthew Restall

This series features primary source texts on colonial and nineteenth-century Latin America, translated into English, in slim, accessible, affordable editions that also make scholarly contributions. Most of these sources are being published in English for the first time and represent an alternative to the traditional texts on early Latin America. The initial focus is on the conquest period in sixteenth-century Spanish America, but subsequent volumes include Brazil and examine later centuries. The series features archival documents and printed sources originally in Spanish, Portuguese, Latin, and various Native American languages. The contributing authors are historians, anthropologists, art historians, and scholars of literature.

Matthew Restall is Edwin Erle Sparks Professor of Latin American History and Anthropology, and Director of Latin American Studies, at the Pennsylvania State University. He edited *Ethnohistory* for a decade and now co-edits the *Hispanic American Historical Review*.